SECTIONAL CRISIS AND SOUTHERN CONSTITUTIONALISM

SECTIONAL CRISIS AND SOUTHERN CONSTITUTIONALISM

Comprising

THE SOUTH AND THREE SECTIONAL CRISES

and

CONSTITUTIONS AND CONSTITUTIONALISM IN THE SLAVEHOLDING SOUTH

with a New Introduction by the Author

Don E. Fehrenbacher

LOUISIANA STATE UNIVERSITY PRESS
Baton Rouge and London

The South and Three Sectional Crises copyright © 1980 by Louisiana State
   University Press
Constitutions and Constitutionalism in the Slaveholding South
   copyright © 1989 by the University of Georgia Press
New material copyright © 1995 by Louisiana State University Press
All rights reserved
Manufactured in the United States of America

Louisiana Paperback Edition, 1995

04 03 02 01 00 99 98 97 96 95   5 4 3 2 1

Fehrenbacher, Don Edward, 1920–
   [South and three sectional crises]
   Sectional crisis and Southern constitutionalism / Don E.
Fehrenbacher. —Louisiana paperback ed.
      p. cm.
   First work originally published: Baton Rouge : Louisiana State
University Press, c1980. Second work originally published: Athens :
University of Georgia Press, c1989.
   Includes bibliographical references and index.
   Contents: The South and three sectional crises. —Constitutions
and constitutionalism in the slaveholding South.
   ISBN 0-8071-2036-7 (pbk. : alk. paper)
   1. Sectionalism (United States)   2. Southern States—
Constitutional history.   3. Missouri compromise.   4. Wilmot
proviso.   5. Kansas—History—1854–1861.   I. Fehrenbacher, Don
Edward, 1920–   Constitutions and constitutionalism in the
slaveholding South.   II. Title.
E338.F44   1995   95-44022
973.7' 133—dc20   CIP

The paper in this book meets the guidelines for permanence and durability
of the Committee on Production Guidelines for Book Longevity of the
Council on Library Resources. ∞

*To my sister and brothers:
Shirley, Bob, and Marvin,
and for Peter and Dottie Foose,
good friends of half a lifetime*

Contents

General Introduction   ix

THE SOUTH AND THREE SECTIONAL CRISES
Preface   xxi
Introduction   1
1 *The Missouri Controversy and the Sources of Southern Sectionalism*   9
2 *The Wilmot Proviso and the Mid-Century Crisis*   25
3 *Kansas, Republicanism, and the Crisis of the Union*   45
Appendix   67
Notes   71

CONSTITUTIONS AND CONSTITUTIONALISM IN THE SLAVEHOLDING SOUTH
Preface   79
1 *Southern State Constitutions*   81
2 *The South and the Federal Constitution*   113
3 *The Confederacy as a Constitutional System*   137
Notes   163

Index   187

General Introduction

One of the enduring consequences of the American Civil War is its profound effect on historical perception of earlier years of the republic. This retrospective influence has always been especially strong in the case of southern history, which is forever anchored, as it were, to Fort Sumter and Appomattox. The war brought the South to its climax as a historical entity. Explicitly or implicitly, all studies of antebellum southern culture are contributions to the history of secession, and all analyses of secession are in some degree explorations of southern culture. Characterization of the South and explanation of the Civil War are interlocking enterprises, with slavery as the heart of the matter in each instance.

In 1787, after instructing members of the Constitutional Convention that the "real difference of interests" in the Union lay between the northern and southern states, James Madison added that "the institution of slavery and its consequences formed the line of distinction." Seventy-eight years later, Abraham Lincoln in his second inaugural address spoke of slavery as "a peculiar and powerful interest" that everyone understood to be "somehow, the cause of the war."[1] Slavery was the principal element distinguishing and integrating the antebellum South, the sole determinant of its boundaries. The terms *South* and *slaveholding* states were synonymous. At the same time, slavery was the primary issue in a series of increasingly dangerous sectional crises, and, indeed, the only thing, as Lincoln said, that ever "threatened the perpetuity of the Union itself."[2] When the final crisis erupted in the winter of 1860-1861, the grievances listed by seceding states were almost entirely concerned with northern hostility to slavery.

To be sure, the center is not the whole. Affirmation of the centrality of slavery is by itself of limited explanatory value, much less satisfactory as a conclusion than as an appropriate starting point for further inquiry into the character of the Old South and the background of the Civil War. So many collateral factors—such as race, economic interest, and social outlook—must be taken into account. So many old traditions and new conditions, so many discrete events and broad cultural trends contributed to the shaping of southern society and the progress of sectional divergence. Adding further complication to the subject is the bulk and interpretive richness of modern scholarship on the slaveholding South. Among other things, the history of slavery itself has been transformed by the use of quantitative methods and by a notable shift of attention to the slave side of the institution. More directly relevant to the sectional conflict is an impressive body of literature exploring white southern values and patterns of thought. For instance, the idea of honor has been elaborately iden-

---

1. Max Farrand, ed., *The Records of the Federal Convention of 1787* (1937, rev. ed., 4 vols.; New Haven, 1966), II, 10; Roy P. Basler *et al.*, eds., *The Collected Works of Abraham Lincoln* (9 vols.; New Brunswick, 1953-55), VIII, 332.
2. Basler *et al.*, eds., *Collected Works of Abraham Lincoln*, III, 460.

tified as the main governing principle of southern life, and the protean concept of republicanism has been adapted to explain why nonslaveholders joined in the secession movement.³

Although recent historical writing about the slaveholding South often seems only vaguely linked to the Civil War, it is in harmony with J. Mills Thornton's view of the war as "the sum of the age," or more specifically as "an outgrowth not merely of the direct sectional encounters, but also of many of the episodes and concerns of the antebellum period which did not have any explicitly sectional content." Acknowledging the importance of the familiar sequence of events running from the Missouri controversy to the election of Lincoln, he maintains that to understand the splash made by a rock thrown into a pond, one must know something about the water as well as the rock.⁴ Innovative and sophisticated studies of the water have indeed yielded splendid returns, but there is much to be said too for periodic reexamination of the rock. One case in point is a pair of books published two decades apart, each of which in its own way significantly revised previous understanding of the Nullification crisis.⁵ The great sectional controversies of the antebellum era are more than dramatic phases of the South's progress toward disunion. They are also revelations of the southern perspective as it changed over time. In intersectional argument, the southerner found it especially

---

3. Bertram Wyatt-Brown, *Southern Honor: Ethics and Behavior in the Old South* (New York, 1982), especially 16, 20, 21–22, 114; Lacy K. Ford, Jr., *Origins of Southern Radicalism: The South Carolina Upcountry, 1800–1860* (New York, 1988), especially viii, 350–52, 360–63, 372.
4. J. Mills Thornton III, *Politics and Power in a Slave Society: Alabama, 1800–1860* (Baton Rouge, 1978), xvii, xxi.
5. William W. Freehling, *Prelude to Civil War: The Nullification Controversy in South Carolina, 1816–1836* (New York, 1966); Richard E. Ellis, *The Union at Risk: Jacksonian Democracy, States' Rights, and the Nullification Crisis* (New York, 1987).

necessary to define himself and his civilization. Congressional debates of a sectional nature, and particularly those concerned with slavery, are consequently a rich source of information on southern beliefs, anxieties, purposes, and codes of behavior.

In the first volume of this twin publication, the three main periods of national crisis over slavery are examined, beginning with the Missouri controversy of 1819–1821. Of course, sectional rivalry in Congress and congressional involvement with slavery antedated 1819. Before that year, however, sectionalism had manifested itself most prominently in connection with other issues (such as federal economic policy and the War of 1812), while slavery legislation (such as reenactment of the Northwest Ordinance and suppression of the foreign slave trade) had been relatively uncontroversial. More inflammatory were several northern attempts to prevent or limit the expansion of slavery into southwestern territory and a southern move to secure passage of a stricter fugitive-slave law, but those efforts had failed.

The fierceness of the Missouri struggle, after a decade in which slavery had been of minor concern in national politics, took political leaders and the American people by surprise. It was as though pent-up feelings on both sides had suddenly burst their confines. For southerners, the emotional consequences of the crisis were long-lasting, and it had a crucial effect on their view of the Federal Union, stimulating a resurgence of states-rights constitutionalism. Southern members of Congress, despite some flights of rhetoric, did not at this time endorse secession as a viable alternative, and only a few of them openly defended slavery as a positive good or denied the power of Congress to exclude it from the territories. But their conduct during the struggle amounted to a virtually unanimous expression of belief in the permanence of slavery, its right to share in national expansion, and its absolute immunity, once established, from constraint or impairment by the federal government.

The Missouri Compromise terminated a dangerous crisis and, by means of the 36° 30′ line, resolved the territorial issue for a quarter of a century. Yet its general pacificatory effect has perhaps been exaggerated. Sectional hostility was not so much reduced as partly diverted into other channels, primarily of an economic nature. Meanwhile, the problem of slavery continued to be a troublesome element in national politics, always rumbling below the surface and sometimes erupting into controversy on the floors of Congress. Among the subjects of extensive and often bitter dispute in the 1820s were American relations with the black republic of Haiti, resolutions looking toward the abolition of slavery and the slave trade in the District of Columbia, proposals for federal assistance to the African Colonization Society, and a bill to remunerate the owner of a slave wounded during the Battle of New Orleans. Soon the rise of the radical abolition movement with its denunciatory style and aggressive strategy opened a new chapter of the slavery controversy. From the mid-1830s onward, disruptive quarrels in Congress, such as those concerning the disposition of abolitionist petitions, became more the rule than the exception.

So the crisis of 1846–1850, unlike the crisis of 1819–1821, followed a decade of continual trouble over slavery. That fact helps explain the intensity of southern reaction to the Wilmot Proviso, a proposal to ban the institution from a region where it seemed unlikely to go anyhow. Outraged by the incessant hammering of abolitionist attacks and fearful that antislavery sentiment was becoming dominant in the North, many southerners were ready for some kind of showdown. For them, defeat of the Proviso was a matter not only of interest and power but of self-respect and honor. By this time, southern spokesmen had fully developed the defensive principle of the "entering wedge," which held that any concession to the critics of slavery would lead to more antislavery demands. Congressmen from the lower and middle South (that is, from the eleven states that would later form the Confederacy) emphatically applied the principle in their votes on the Compromise of 1850, 85 percent of them opposing the admission of California as a free state and 94 percent of them opposing the bill to limit the sale of slaves in the District of Columbia. Although the crisis nevertheless ended in a semblance of compromise, its most significant feature turned out to be the emergence of a real secession movement—one that was spearheaded by a relatively small number of fire-eaters but came to have much broader appeal as a contingent alternative for the embattled South.

Secessionism was a brooding presence throughout the final phase of the sectional conflict, which comprised a number of separate confrontations and two basic kinds of crisis, one familiarly congressional and the other ominously electoral. A violent struggle over slavery in Kansas that began in 1854 with repeal of the 36° 30' restriction was settled four years later in one last, rather sleazy legislative compromise. But out of that controversy rose the country's first major political party with an antislavery agenda, and slaveholders now faced the possibility of having an avowed enemy in the White House. The presidential election of 1856 was therefore something of a secession crisis, and the election of 1860 proved to be one beyond the reach of all strategies and agents of compromise.

Because of the obvious connection between the emergence of Republicanism and the disruption of the Union, as well as the fact that the subject lends itself admirably to quantitative treatment, the party revolution of the 1850s has received an extraordinary amount of scholarly attention in recent decades. The general effect has been to lay more emphasis on ethnocultural factors and somewhat diminish the importance of the slavery issue as a primary cause of the political upheaval.[6] Nevertheless, however complex its origins, the Republican party soon coalesced as a strictly antislavery organization, and what proved to be crucial in any case was southern *perception* of the party as the advance echelon of abolitionist fanaticism.

Detailed accounts of the secession movement, whatever their vintage, serve to remind us that the words *South* and *southerner* are abstractions covering a wide variety of places, people, and points of view. Unlike the issue of slavery, which tended to unify the South, the question of disunion exposed and accentuated its internal differences. Secessionism did not have equal appeal among urban and rural southerners, for example, or among slaveholding and nonslaveholding southerners, or among Democratic and former Whig southerners. But of course the most conspicuous line of division in the winter of 1860–1861 separated the seven southern states that seceded in response to Lincoln's election from the eight that did not. It was the lower South that made secession a reality, created the Confederate States of America, and launched the new nation into war. Virginia and Tennessee, where Civil War battlefields are thickest, played no part in those decisions and undertakings. Yet for viewing the complexities of the political situation and the

---

6. See, for example, William E. Gienapp, *The Origins of the Republican Party, 1852–1856* (New York, 1987), especially 443–48.

alternatives fleetingly available, there is perhaps no better standpoint than the four states of the middle South, which first rejected secession but then embraced it after the dramatic turn of events at Fort Sumter.[7]

In this final crisis of the Union, as in earlier sectional confrontations, the debate often ran along constitutional lines. The compromise package proposed and defeated in the Senate consisted of six constitutional amendments, plus four resolutions—all dealing with slavery. By the time Lincoln took office, the critical focus had shifted from slavery to the right of secession, but the Civil War permanently resolved both issues and thus, even without taking the Fourteenth Amendment into account, may be said to have had momentous constitutional consequences. May it also be said to have sprung in some part from constitutional causes? Is there any merit in Alexander H. Stephens' later assertion that the fundamental matter in dispute between North and South was not slavery but "the very nature and organic structure of the government"?[8] Constitutional argument is commonly regarded as shadow rather than substance, as rationalization or forensic strategy rather than revelation of motive or statement of real purpose. Still, as Arthur Bestor pointed out many years ago, constitutional ideas and arrangements can have "a powerful shaping effect upon the course that events will in actuality take." Thus, it was "constitutional theorizing, carried on from the very birth of the Republic, which made secession the ultimate recourse of any group that considered its vital interests threatened."[9]

---

7. See Daniel W. Crofts, *Reluctant Confederates: Upper South Unionists in the Secession Crisis* (Chapel Hill, 1989).

8. Alexander H. Stephens, *A Constitutional View of the Late War Between the States* (2 vols.; Philadelphia, 1868–70), I, 12.

9. Arthur Bestor, "The American Civil War as a Constitutional Crisis," *American Historical Review*, LXIX (1963–64), 329.

Constitutional perspective, whatever the estimate of its influence on specific events, was certainly a key element in the political culture of the antebellum South, one that is particularly relevant when discussion turns to the nature and degree of southern distinctiveness.

In the second volume of this twin publication, three aspects of southern constitutionalism are examined, beginning with southern state constitutions as they developed from the Revolution to the Civil War. State constitutional history, though receiving some stimulus from the hearty growth of legal history and from the bicentennial scholarship of the 1980s, continues to be a lightly cultivated field of study—surprisingly so in view of the fact that state constitutions were the original models of American constitutionalism and have "historically provided much of the grist for the nation's rich constitutional politics."[10] Perhaps the outstanding feature of state constitutional development in the slaveholding South was its similarity to such development elsewhere.[11] Thus, southern states, like northern states, began with something approaching legislative supremacy and, except for South Carolina, moved at varying speeds toward greater executive and judicial independence—that is, toward realizing the principle of separation of powers. Also, many southern states, like many northern states, lengthened their constitutions to deal more elaborately with the structure of government and more emphatically with certain matters of public policy. And, as time passed, constitutions north and south came to reflect the democratic tendencies

10. Kermit L. Hall, "The Irony of the Federal Constitution's Genius: State Constitutional Development," in *The Constitution and American Political Development: An Institutional Perspective* , ed. Peter F. Nardulli (Urbana; 1992), 235–36.

11. Daniel J. Elazar's differentiation of southern constitutions under the label "contractual pattern" does not seem to have a great deal of substance with respect to the South before Reconstruction. Elazar, "The Principles and Traditions Underlying State Constitutions," *Publius*, XII (1982), 20–21.

of the age with suffrage broadened and appointive offices made elective. Eminently bisectional, for example, was the antebellum trend toward an elective judiciary of limited tenure, a trend that began in Mississippi in 1832 and reached its climax during the 1850s. Perhaps in no other respect did American state government take so sharp a turn away from the national model. Contemporary opponents and later critics commonly regarded the change as Jacksonian democracy carried emotionally to excess. In recent scholarship, it is treated more sympathetically, either as a calculated effort to rein in legislative power by improving the prestige of the judiciary or as a classic republican expression of distrust for all official power.[12]

The democratization of state judiciaries occurred at a time when judicial power to invalidate legislation on grounds of unconstitutionality was becoming firmly established at the state as well as the national level. To be sure, despite the fame of *Marbury v. Madison* and *Dred Scott v. Sandford*, "co-ordinate" judicial review (federal court review of federal law and state court review of state law) did not significantly affect the making of public policy. More influential was federal court review of state law, a jurisprudence always addressed in one way or another to the problem of federal relations. In that day, however, constitutional questions were not viewed as peculiarly judicial questions, and constitutional argument about the federal system was no doubt more common in legislatures and other political arenas than in courts of law.

12. Kermit L. Hall, "The Judiciary on Trial: State Constitutional Reform and the Rise of an Elected Judiciary, 1846–1860," *Historian*, XLV (1982–83), 337–54; Caleb Nelson, "A Re-Evaluation of Scholarly Explanations for the Rise of the Elective Judiciary in Antebellum America," *American Journal of Legal History*, XXXVII (1993), 190–224.

If the history of state constitutional development seems to place the antebellum South in the American mainstream, the southern conception of the Federal Union, especially as it was articulated by John C. Calhoun, serves to exemplify and dramatize southern separatism. States-rights constitutionalism, which became identified peculiarly with the South after 1820, was a logical defensive posture for a minority section conscious of its growing vulnerability as a slaveholding society. The doctrine of state sovereignty and the concept of the "concurrent majority" were the twin fundamentals of a political theory aimed at neutralizing the tyrannical strength of the majority by investing constituent communities or interests with some kind of veto power. The presumed effect would be consensual government, or something approaching it, instead of naked majority rule.[13] Ostensibly formulated as an alternative to disunion, Calhoun's theory nevertheless pointed in the direction of secession, at least as a last resort. What complicated matters and helped postpone the southern hour of decision was the operation of the national party system, which enabled the South, even as its minority status became increasingly evident, to continue playing a dominant role in the exercise of majority power. When that advantage began to crumble in the late 1850s, the disruptive potential of states-rights constitutionalism came fully into play.

Southern constitutional theory led, not inevitably but circumstantially, to secession, which in turn led to a new exper-

---

13. Although Calhoun used both principles to justify nullification, he defined and illustrated "concurrent majority" in other contexts besides that of the federal-state relationship. See Clyde N. Wilson, ed., *The Papers of John C. Calhoun,* Vol. XI (Columbia, S.C., 1978), 254–55; Vol. XII (1979), 84–85, 90–91, 134; Richard K. Calle, ed., *The Works of John C. Calhoun* (6 vols.; New York, 1888), I, 25, 28–73, 91–106. For the Madisonian background of the concept, see Lacy K. Ford, Jr., "Inventing the Concurrent Majority: Madison, Calhoun, and the Problem of Majoritarianism in American Political Thought," *Journal of Southern History,* LX (1994), 19–58.

iment in the creation of a federal republic. The Confederate Constitution, though functionally short-lived, has unique historical value as a formal statement of what southerners wanted to leave behind and what they wanted to take with them when they departed from their old allegiance. For one thing, of course, they wanted to leave behind all doubts about the future of slavery, and so, to no one's surprise, they established a nation in which the institution was given full constitutional sanction. More intriguing are other parts of the new constitution, such as a clause limiting the president's power of appointment, which bespoke a general hostility to political parties. In fact, the antiparty aroma of the document is so strong that one historian has recently labeled the entire Confederate enterprise "a revolution against politics."[14] The extent to which such distrust of parties was peculiarly southern, the extent to which it reflected the persistence of eighteenth-century republican ideology, the extent to which the revulsion stemmed from southern political experiences in the 1850s and was related to the genesis of southern nationalism—all are matters of continuing scholarly discussion.

Yet in spite of these and other substantial changes, the most striking thing about the Confederate Constitution was its resemblance to the Constitution of the United States. Innovative in certain respects and adapted to an officially proslavery purpose, it was nevertheless essentially a document of retention, looking reverently backward to the foundations of the American nation. In its text one finds the combination of venturousness and conservatism that created the Confederacy, as well as the special blend of national and distinctively regional identity characteristic of the slaveholding South.

14. George C. Rable, *The Confederate Republic: A Revolution Against Politics* (Chapel Hill, 1994).

The South and Three Sectional Crises

Preface

One writes a lecture listening to the sound of it, knowing that the words will be heard before they are read. Clarity and liveliness are at a premium; comprehensiveness is usually out of the question; and accuracy may suffer—especially the kind of accuracy that qualifies every generalization and rehearses the complexities of the subject. There is consequently much to be said for revising and expanding lectures before committing them to print, but in this instance I have chosen to forego the opportunity. The reason, quite simply, is diffidence in the face of the accumulated complexity of the literature on the causes of the Civil War. That is, I have been governed by the expectation that any such enterprise of expansion, once begun, might be extremely difficult to terminate. Except, then, for some changes of a formal nature (such as separating my introductory remarks from the body of the first lecture), the following pages reproduce my three Walter Lynwood Fleming Lectures in Southern History, just as I presented them at Louisiana State University on April 17 and 18, 1978. For the warm hospitality extended to me and my wife on that occasion, I thank the University and its Department of History, and particularly John L. and Helen Loos and Mark T. and Maureen Carleton. I am also grateful to Lewis P. Simpson for arranging publication of the first lecture in the *Southern Review*. In preparing the book for publication, I have had, as usual, much help from my wife Virginia, and I have enjoyed the gracious cooperation of the staff of the LSU Press.

Introduction

My sectional credentials for the occasion were not impressive. Born in Illinois of parents likewise born in Illinois, I was educated in Illinois and Iowa and have lived for the past quarter of a century in California (not even Southern California at that). As a historian, I have written much more about Abraham Lincoln than about Jefferson Davis or Robert E. Lee. *And* my great-grandfather, Corporal George W. Outman of the 73rd Regiment of Illinois Volunteer Infantry, was killed by a Rebel sniper on New Year's Eve, 1862, leaving behind him a widow and three small children. Nevertheless, despite this inappropriate personal background, I recently had the honor of delivering the thirty-ninth Walter Lynwood Fleming Lectures in Southern History at Louisiana State University. It is no doubt safe to say that such a thing could happen only in America.

Let it be added, however, that I can claim one important southern connection. In graduate school at the University of Chicago, my teacher and dissertation director was a famous historian of the South, Avery O. Craven—the only scholar to serve twice as the Fleming Lecturer. His first series of lectures, presented in 1938 and entitled "The Repressible Conflict," became a landmark in the historiography of the Civil War. Returning in 1958, he addressed himself to the same subject with the title "Civil War in the Making"; for Craven was, of all American historians, the most persistent in his efforts to understand the disruption of the Union. Thus, in 1978, forty years after his first appearance as Fleming Lecturer and twenty years after his second, it seemed appropriate that one of Avery Craven's students should likewise venture a brief exploration of that treacherous scholar's jungle, the background of the Civil War.

Study of the subject is no longer as fashionable as it was when Craven, James G. Randall, Allan Nevins, Roy F. Nichols, David M. Potter, Kenneth M. Stampp, and others were all working the vein of historical ore that runs from the Wilmot Proviso to the firing on Fort Sumter; when the forays of Bernard DeVoto, Arthur M. Schlesinger, Jr., Frank L. Owsley, and Pieter Geyl were enlivening the tangled argument over causation; and when every scholar in the field was expected to take a stand on the question of whether the Civil War was or was not avoidable.

The battle of interpretations ran its course, becoming increasingly recapitulative and sterile. Civil War causation lost much of its intellectual appeal, and in 1960 David Herbert Donald pronounced it "dead" as a subject of scholarly investigation.[1] Four years later, at the age of seventy-eight, Avery Craven wryly acknowledged the "futility of trying to understand and explain the causes of the American Civil War."[2] At about the same time, Joel H. Silbey, speaking as a practitioner of the so-called "new political history," declared that scholarly emphasis on the coming of the Civil War had perniciously "distorted the reality" of antebellum politics by exaggerating the incidence and influence of sectional rivalry.[3]

In 1974, Eric Foner, after noting the impressive quantity and quality of recent scholarship on racism, slavery, and abolitionism, nevertheless concluded that explanation of the coming of the Civil War had made little progress since Donald's pronouncement in 1960. The problem, in his view, was poverty of conceptualization. "Discussion of the causes of the Civil War," he wrote, "continues to be locked into an antiquated interpretive framework. Historians of the Civil War era seem to be in greater need of new models of interpretation and new questions than of an additional accumulation of data." As an example of the kind of innovative thinking that is needed, Foner pointed to the concept of "modernization" and more specifically to the view of the Civil War as "the process by which the 'modern' or 'modernizing' North integrated the 'pre-modern' South into a national political and economic system."[4]

Such new models of interpretation for old historical problems are often synthetic and modish, however, reflecting the latest fashions in behavioral science theory and terminology but adding little to the substance of explanation. The concept of "modernization," in so far as it can be used to explain the coming of the Civil War, was largely anticipated by Avery Craven in sentences like this one written in 1964: "The real tragedy lies in the fact that these people [that is, the people of the antebellum South] remained socially and intellectually *comfortably* where they were, while the whole Western world, of which cotton made them a part, rushed headlong into the modern world of nationalism, industrial capitalism, democratic advancement, and a new respect for human rights."[5]

One virtue of the modernization model, according to Foner, is that it "enables us to see that what happened in nineteenth century America was not a unique or local occurrence, but a process which had deep affinities with events in many other areas of the world."[6] Yet the American experience was in some respects unique; for, as Carl N. Degler wrote in 1970: "The United States is the only country that required a civil war to eradicate slavery."[7] In short, the concept of "modernization," with its wide range of implications (including industrialization, urbanization, national integration, and psychological adaptation to rapid social change) may help us to understand why American slavery came to an end, but not why it came to a violent end.

What caused the Civil War is not a single historical problem but rather a whole cluster of problems, too numerous and complex to be incorporated into any single model of historical interpretation. For example, one crucial question, which has been answered most fully by David Brion Davis, is why Negro slavery, after several hundred years of respectable existence, suddenly came under fierce moral attack.[8] But no explanation of the origins of abolitionism will suffice to explain the emergence of a mass antislavery political organization in the 1850s. And, in turn, satisfactory reasons for the birth of the Republican party would not be enough to explain the Republican electoral triumph in 1860.

No more than the coming of the French Revolution is the coming of the American Civil War likely to be abandoned as a subject of historical inquiry in the lifetime of anyone now living; for there continues to be a great emotional investment in remembrance of the conflict, and every generation of Americans seems to discover some new understanding of itself in studying the spectacular and tragic disruption of the American Union. As for making progress toward better causal explanation, perhaps it is less important to invent new questions than to phrase some of the old questions more carefully and pursue the answers more diligently and rigorously.

Most discussion of the causes of the Civil War tends to concentrate on the causes of southern secession, in spite of the fact that armed conflict actually resulted from northern unwillingness to acquiesce in peaceable separation. Explanation of secession, though by no means the whole of the matter, is undoubtedly the heart of the matter. For secession was the most venturesome and extraordinary action in the sectional crisis— the one requiring the greatest amount of initiative—the biggest step into the unknown. But precisely what is meant by the term "southern secession"? The author of a recently published book falls into a common habit when he speaks of "the exuberance and confidence with which the South seceded."[9] The South, of course, did not secede. It was South Carolina that did so— South Carolina alone, followed in order by Mississippi, Florida, and Alabama; then by Georgia, Louisiana, and Texas; and later, after the guns had sounded in Charleston Harbor, by Virginia, Arkansas, Tennessee, and North Carolina. In addition, Kentucky and Missouri were claimed as parts of the Confederacy, but they are generally counted with Delaware and Maryland among the slaveholding states that did not secede at all.

The Civil War was precipitated, then, by the secession of just seven state governments, acting sequentially and representing less than one-third of the free population of the entire South. The number of secessions before Lincoln's inauguration probably fell within a critical range as far as the danger of war was concerned. That is, if only three or four states had seceded, such a feeble effort might well have ended peacefully in failure, whereas, if twelve or thirteen states had seceded before Lincoln's inauguration, such a formidable movement might well have ended peacefully in success. It is possible that seven was the optimum number of secessions for starting a civil war, and it may be that Virginia's initial failure to secede was as much a cause of war as South Carolina's headlong leadership in the secession movement.

Therefore, in explaining the causes of the Civil War, perhaps one ought to emphasize secessionism in seven of the southern states and antisecessionism in the other eight. Certainly there is good reason to differentiate southern states according to their behavior in the secession crisis and then keep the principal categories strictly in mind throughout any study of the sectional conflict. Those categories are: the seven states of the Lower

South that seceded after Lincoln's election; the four states of the Middle South that seceded after the firing on Fort Sumter; and the four states of the Border South that did not secede at all. In these three regions respectively, slaves were 46 percent, 29 percent, and 14 percent of the total population.[10] Of course the Lower South and Middle South together made up the Confederate South. The eight states of the Middle and Border Souths combined may be called the Upper South. And all three regions taken together constituted the fifteen states of the Slaveholding South.

There is another, more abstract problem of method that I would like to discuss before proceeding to a review of southern participation in the three great sectional crises of 1819–1821, 1846–1850, and 1854–1861. Avery Craven sometimes insisted that his purpose was not to explain the causes of the Civil War but rather merely to explain "how events got into such shape that they could not be handled by the democratic process."[11] Critics did not take the protestation very seriously, and Craven himself repeatedly blurred the distinction he sought to draw. A differentiation between *causes* and the *shape of events* may be unsound and ultimately unmanageable, but it has a special usefulness as a way of looking at the background of the Civil War.

Craven was talking about the problem of how historical causes are so activated as to produce their consequences—how attitudes and purposes are crystallized into action. The Civil War had no real equivalent of the skirmishes at Lexington and Concord. It did not flare up out of local violence and spread across the land. Apparently there was never much danger that it *would* begin in such a way—not even as a result of John Brown's inflammatory adventure at Harpers Ferry. The accumulation of sectional hostility in antebellum America was translated into civil war through the intermedium of secession. And secession, though fraught with passion, was nevertheless not only nonviolent but highly formal. So formal, in fact, as to increase substantially the difficulty of setting it in motion. Secession could not be provoked by any informal outburst of sectional animosity, such as that associated with the Harpers Ferry raid, but only by a formal public act or action of major import, such as passage of a federal law. The famous Georgia platform of 1850 listed six eventualities, any one of which would be sufficient cause for disunion, and all six were apprehended actions of Congress.[12]

We might therefore visualize the accumulating sectional hostility as a charge of explosive that grew to be enormous in its destructive potential but was never extremely unstable. It could not be set off by a random spark like a dust-filled grain elevator. Instead, the explosion required the formality of a detonator or fuse. I believe that Craven's distinction between causes and the shape of events was essentially a distinction between charge and fuse. I also believe that the highly formal nature of secession makes the distinction especially helpful in study of the coming of the Civil War; for in a sense the decisive change that took place in the late 1850s was not the ominous continuing increase in the size of the charge, but rather the introduction of a new and more effective fuse.

1 The Missouri Controversy and the Sources of Southern Sectionalism

Historians generally agree that the Missouri controversy of 1819–1821 was a turning point in the history of the sectional conflict, but they differ about what phase it constituted in the development of southern distinctiveness and self-awareness. James A. Woodburn called the struggle "the first clear demarcation between the sections."[1] Clement Eaton said that in political terms, the South "did not begin until 1820."[2] Charles S. Sydnor suggested that it might be anachronistic to use the word "southerners" for the time before 1819; for, as he put it, "regional differences had not borne the evil fruit of sectional bitterness."[3] On the other hand, Jesse T. Carpenter dated his study of *The South as a Conscious Minority* from the year 1789 and insisted, indeed, that "the inhabitants of those states below the Mason and Dixon line always considered themselves a separate and distinct people."[4] Also, John R. Alden in his Fleming Lectures undertook to demonstrate the historical reality of what he called the First South. "It appeared," he said, "with the American nation; it was christened as early as 1778; and it clashed ever more sharply with a First North during and immediately after the War of Independence."[5]

The disagreement between these scholars is partly one of their criteria and emphases, but it also reflects a cyclical pattern in the awakening of the South. That is, to some historians the Missouri Compromise looks like the beginning of southern sectionalism because in certain respects it was a *new* beginning of that phenomenon.

The underlying social and economic differences between the northern and southern colonies inspired open political rivalry from the formation of the Republic; and political rivalry, in turn, was the principal stimulant of sectional consciousness. In 1776, during early stages of work on the Articles of Confederation, members of the Continental Congress engaged in a sharp debate on the question of whether slaves should be counted in the apportionment of taxes. The division was almost totally along sectional lines. The same issue, tied to the problem of representation in Congress, troubled the deliberations of the Constitutional Convention in 1787, until the matter was at last settled by adoption of the three-fifths compromise. Yet slavery, though defended vehemently at times, especially by representatives of South Carolina and Georgia, was not the primary subject of contention between North and South during the first quarter century of independence.

More serious were the sectional quarrels over navigation of the Mississippi River, over Alexander Hamilton's financial program for the new nation, and over Jay's treaty with Great Britain, negotiated in 1794. Mounting southern opposition to the Federalist regime stemmed primarily from the conviction that national policies were favoring northern commercial enterprise at the expense of southern agriculture. "We are completely under the saddle of Massachusetts and Connecticut," said Thomas Jefferson in 1798. "They ride us very hard, cruelly insulting our feelings as well as exhausting our strength and subsistence."[6] The emergence of the Jeffersonian Republican opposition as an organized political party was to no small degree a sectional event. In the presidential election of 1796, Jefferson won fifty out of fifty-two electoral votes in the states south of Maryland; John Adams won all fifty-one electoral votes in the states north of Pennsylvania; and the thirty-six votes of New Jersey, Pennsylvania, Delaware, and Maryland were divided equally between them.

One way that the sectionalism of the 1790s foreshadowed the sectionalism of the 1850s was in the widespread fear of conspiracy on both sides. The Alien and Sedition acts confirmed many Republicans in their suspicion of a Federalist design to crush freedom of dissent and establish a monarchy. Jefferson predicted that the next step would be an attempt to make Adams president for life.[7] On the other hand, the famous resolutions of Virginia and Kentucky attacking the Alien and Sedition acts only strengthened the conviction of many Federalists that Republican leaders were engaged in a treasonable plot to overthrow the Constitution and turn the United States into an appendage of Revolutionary France.

Within this context of intense partisan conflict, southerners in the 1790s did indeed have a growing sense of being mistreated as a section (though not on account of slavery), and their protests sometimes had the ring of prophecy. The Virginia and Kentucky Resolutions laid out the doctrines of strict construction, state sovereignty, and nullification. And among some Virginians there was apparently talk of secession and even of armed resistance to federal power. But the resolutions were not intended as blueprints for any organized southern action, except action at the polls. They were, in practical terms, campaign literature. Jefferson's goal was not a united South but control of the federal government. When that was achieved in 1800, much of the reason for southern sectionalism disappeared, and New England became the nation's conscious minority, ridden hard under a Virginia saddle.

With southern political power ascendant, the Jeffersonian

era was a period without parallel in the territorial expansion of slavery. Jefferson himself did little to prevent it, and, in fact, he came to embrace the popular southern argument that a wide diffusion of slavery would benefit the slave population and the nation as a whole. In 1784, he had proposed that the institution be prohibited in the entire trans-Appalachian West, but as president he made no effort to secure the exclusion of slavery from the Louisiana Purchase. On the contrary, the plan for the government of Louisiana that he sent to Congress in November 1803 included a rigorous slave code.[8]

Like a good many other enlightened Virginians of the Revolutionary generation, Jefferson had long since gone inactive in his opposition to slavery. Racial preconceptions and fears, as well as political considerations, had blunted his lifelong hatred of the institution and driven him to the conviction that the problem could be solved only by the slow working of time.[9] He headed a political party of predominantly southern interest, but one that needed northern allies to control the presidency and Congress. The Jeffersonian Republicans, like their successors the Jacksonian Democrats, accordingly had good reason to muffle the issue of slavery, and northern members of the party were under strong though usually tacit pressure to restrain whatever antislavery feelings they may have had.

The Jeffersonian silence on domestic slavery was not sectionally neutral in its effect on westward expansion; for previous legislation dating back to 1790 had established the rule that slaveholding could be practiced anywhere in federal territory if it was not positively forbidden by federal law. This was doubly true of Louisiana, where slavery had been legal under both French and Spanish dominion. The Jeffersonians were consequently able to legitimate slaveholding throughout the whole of Louisiana simply by passing territorial organic acts that contained no provisions excluding it.

The strongest antislavery resistance arose in 1804. A proposal to limit (but not to abolish) slavery in Orleans Territory was defeated in the Senate by a vote of seventeen to eleven, with northern Federalists and northern Republicans both fairly evenly divided, while southerners provided the margin of defeat. During the next fifteen years, slavery continued to expand across the Mississippi as far north as St. Louis, without provoking sectional controversy.[10]

Furthermore, slavery in several other respects seemed securely linked to the nation's destiny. The vitality of the institution was indicated by its continued existence in Illinois and Indiana more than thirty years after it had been officially prohibited there. Southerners could take their household slaves with them into free states for extended visits—up to nine months by law in New York, for example. The national capital was a slaveholding community, with a slave code enforced by federal authority, and the United States, in its relations with foreign powers, conducted itself as a slaveholding nation. The very power and respectability of the slavery interest, which had not been seriously challenged for more than a decade, made the shock of the Missouri crisis all the greater for southerners when it came.

Just why northern members of Congress, after so many years of passivity, chose to take a stand in 1819 is still an open question among historians. As late as April 1818, a proposal to forbid slavery in all states thereafter admitted was quickly smothered in the House of Representatives.[11] Yet, within ten months, antislavery sentiment had swept into control of the chamber and precipitated the first sectional crisis over slavery. It did make a difference, of course, to have the War of 1812 ended and Europe generally at peace after a quarter century of upheaval and conflict. With American interest turning inward after 1815, a renewal of national self-scrutiny was bound to include consideration of the paradox of slavery in a nation formally dedicated to the principle that all men are created equal. Many northern congressmen seem to have awakened more or less suddenly to a realization that slavery had come to be fearfully predominant in the design of the nation's future. For confirmation they needed only to look at the boundaries proposed for the new state of Missouri, which would carry the institution northward two hundred miles above the mouth of the Ohio River.

To be sure, political motives also played their part. Jefferson's overwrought suspicion, shared by Madison and Monroe, that the Missouri controversy sprang from Federalist ambition to regain power, was not entirely groundless. Yet a Federalist effort alone could not have produced a crisis. It was the antislavery solidarity of so many northern Republicans that dismayed the South and inspired a new surge in the development of southern consciousness. The weakness of Federalism as a national party had slackened the need for loyalty and discipline within the Republican organization, thus making members of Congress more amenable to sectional pressures. It was not just accident that the Missouri crisis coincided with the demise of the first American party system.[12]

In spite of Jefferson's famous comparison of the crisis to "a fire bell in the night," there were some intimations in 1818 of what was soon to come. An attempt to pass a more stringent fugitive-slave law ended in failure, but not before it had provoked a good deal of sectional feeling. Later in the year, Congressman James Tallmadge, Jr., spoke out against a bill admitting Illinois to statehood. He argued that slavery was not "sufficiently prohibited" in the Illinois constitution, and about one-third of the northern congressmen joined him in voting against admission.[13]

It was this same James Tallmadge, a New York Republican of the disaffected Clintonian faction, who set off the Missouri struggle in February 1819. To a proposed enabling act for Missouri, he offered an amendment prohibiting the further introduction of slavery and providing that slave children born after the date of admission should be free at the age of twenty-five. Note that Tallmadge was not proposing emancipation of the ten thousand slaves already held in Missouri. His amendment amounted to a program of gradual abolition that would have extended over more than half a century.

With southern members almost unanimous in their opposition, the House of Representatives approved both parts of the Tallmadge proviso.[14] What followed is a familiar chapter in American history. The Senate struck the proviso from the bill. The House refused to concur. The Senate insisted, and again the House refused to concur. Congress adjourned in March with the issue unsettled and the angry debate resounding across the country. A new Congress convened in December 1819, but the two houses quickly discovered that they were no nearer agreement on the Missouri question. After more than two months of further debate, a compromise package was put together and approved in the Senate, then accepted piecemeal by the House. It comprised the admission of Maine as a free state and an enabling act for Missouri without restriction on slavery, together with the provision that in the remaining federal territory acquired from France, slavery should be "forever prohibited" north of latitude 36° 30'.[15]

The crisis accordingly appeared to be at an end, but it was furiously renewed a year later when Missouri applied for admission with a constitution that forbade free Negroes to enter the state. Again, heated debate extended over several months. Maine having already been admitted to statehood, southerners accused northerners of bad faith in setting up an additional barrier to the admission of Missouri. At last both houses of Congress accepted the terms of a second Missouri Compromise, which ambiguously guaranteed citizens the right to enter Missouri without saying whether free blacks were citizens.[16]

In many obvious ways, the two-year struggle anticipated

the sectional argument and the sectional anger of the late antebellum period, but it is important to note differences as well as similarities. The first Missouri controversy, in 1819–1820, was primarily over the power of Congress to set conditions on the admission of a state. The second, in 1821, was over the rights of free Negroes. As for the issue that would later preoccupy so much public discussion—namely, the power of Congress over slavery in the territories—it never assumed critical importance and rose when it did chiefly in connection with Arkansas, rather than in the Missouri debates. Legislation for the organization of Arkansas Territory, made necessary by the prospective admission of Missouri, proceeded through Congress virtually in tandem with the ill-fated Missouri bill of 1819. Discussion of the two measures became somewhat intermixed because antislavery leaders tried several times without success to fasten the Tallmadge restrictions on Arkansas.

Now, the Missouri debate tended to be heavily constitutional, involving several fundamental questions about the relationship between federal power and state sovereignty. And to some extent this tendency spilled over into the debate on Arkansas. Previously, the constitutional authority of Congress over slavery in the territories (which rested, after all, on a body of legislative precedent dating back to the Northwest Ordinance) had never been significantly challenged. During the Arkansas debate and even at some points in the Missouri controversy, a number of southerners did question that authority, and a few, like the future president John Tyler, emphatically denied it.[17] These were but random beginnings, however, of the great constitutional debate that would convulse the nation by midcentury. In 1819, southern congressmen relied more on other arguments, such as economic necessity and sectional equity, to justify slaveholding in Arkansas. Probably a majority of them still had little doubt of congressional power to exclude slavery from the territories, and, indeed, many of them implicitly acknowledged the power by voting for the 36° 30' restriction.

The efforts in the House of Representatives to impose antislavery restrictions on Arkansas Territory failed by very narrow margins. The House passed the territorial organization bill and sent it on to the Senate just three days after having passed and sent on the Missouri enabling bill with the Tallmadge amendment attached. By making no attempt to unite the two measures, antislavery leaders in the House neglected an opportunity to use slavery in Arkansas as leverage against slavery in Missouri. The Senate simply passed the Arkansas bill (which was then signed into law by President James Monroe) while refusing to accept the Missouri bill unless the Tallmadge amendment were deleted. When a similar opportunity presented itself to the Senate a year later, there was no hesitation about using the admission of Maine as leverage against slavery restrictions on Missouri. More often than not in later times of sectional crisis, the power advantage of an antislavery majority in the House of Representatives would be neutralized by the superior parliamentary skills of its adversaries.

For that matter, the Missouri Compromise of 1820 was, in behavioral terms, no compromise at all but essentially a caving-in of the House's slender antislavery majority that had managed to block passage of the Missouri bill for more than a year. Southerners, in contrast, never failed to present a solid front where Missouri was concerned. On the crucial proposal to strike out the slavery restriction (which finally passed the House with just one vote to spare), combined voting of both houses, broken down by sections, was: northern members, 19 in favor and 102 against; southern members, 98 in favor and *none* against.[18]

In a sense, then, the only real compromisers were those nineteen northern members of Congress—and more particularly, the fourteen in the House—who forced their section to yield on the critical issue. But assignment of responsibility for the Missouri Compromise is not so easily accomplished. To begin with, there is a problem of terminology. The admission of Maine in 1820 and Missouri in 1821, being irrevocable acts of Congress, quickly faded from public controversy and became matters of settled history instead. In later years, accordingly, the phrase "Missouri Compromise" was often used to designate only that part of the settlement of 1820 that remained operative —namely, the 36° 30' restriction by itself. Historians have generally followed the same practice. For instance, the Kansas-Nebraska Act of 1854 is commonly spoken of as having repealed the Missouri Compromise, whereas it actually repealed only the 36° 30' restriction. This confusion of terms has led some scholars to the mistaken belief that congressmen from the free states were the principal authors of compromise, for the sectional voting on the 36° 30' restriction in both houses combined was: northern members, 115 in favor and 7 opposed; southern members, 53 in favor and 45 opposed.[19] But the 36° 30' restriction was actually just one-half of one side of the compromise. A grossly uneven division of the remaining federal territory, it had been proposed originally during the Arkansas debates by John W. Taylor, an antislavery Republican from New York. Later, however, it was brought forward by proslavery strategists as a concession to the North—as part of the price to be paid for the admission of Missouri as a slaveholding state.

Of course the real compromise, if there really *was* a compromise, consisted of the Missouri bill, the Maine bill, and the 36° 30' restriction. Sectional attitudes are especially clear in the proceedings of the Senate, where the three measures were at one point voted on as a single package. Southerners supported the package, 20 to 2; northerners opposed it, 18 to 4. "The vote," says Glover Moore, "leaves no doubt about which section of the country favored and which did not favor the compromise of 1820."[20] But the vote does *not* mean that southern members of Congress were generally more reasonable and flexible than their northern colleagues. It means only that in this *particular* compromise plan, formulated by proslavery leaders, the South got what it wanted most and the North did not. The contest from the beginning was for the future of Missouri, with the 36° 30' restriction added as a consolation prize.

In retrospect, southern willingness to surrender the vast area north of 36° 30' is somewhat surprising. No doubt it reflected a low estimate of the region's potential value, especially for plantation agriculture. But in addition, most southerners and northerners alike seem to have been convinced that the Missouri bird in the hand was worth more than several birds in the territorial bush.

In the House of Representatives, where no vote was ever taken on the Compromise as a whole, the vote on the 36° 30' restriction provides the best measure, though an imprecise one, of various attitudes within the southern delegation.[21] Southern representatives supported the restriction by the narrow margin of 39 to 37. The three border states (Delaware, Maryland, and Kentucky) voted 16 to 2 in favor; Virginia, 18 to 4 against; and the rest of the South, 19 to 17 in favor, with South Carolina contributing five affirmative votes and four negative ones.

Thus the center of proslavery extremism in 1820 was not the Lower South but Virginia, aptly described by Glover Moore as "a nation within a nation, eager to maintain its prestige and prerogatives."[22] Thomas Ritchie's Richmond *Enquirer* led the newspaper attack on the Compromise, insisting that the South must not allow itself to be browbeaten by the antislavery forces into ransoming Missouri by consenting to the 36° 30' restriction. "Shall we," the *Enquirer* asked, "surrender so much of this region, that was nobly won by the councils of a Jefferson, and paid for out of a common treasury?" Warning that the precedent set would invite further sectional aggression, it added: "If we yield now, beware.—they will ride us forever." The *En-*

quirer greeted passage of the Compromise in March 1820 with the words, "We scarcely ever recollect to have tasted of a bitterer cup. . . . The door is henceforth slammed in our faces. . . . What is a *territorial* restriction to-day becomes a *state* restriction to-morrow."[23]

The 36° 30' restriction, though opposed by many southerners, provoked very little debate in either house. The restriction was not needed to get the Missouri bill through the Senate, and there is no clear evidence that it changed a single northern vote in the House of Representatives. As a generous concession to antislavery sentiment, it made things much easier for history's original "doughfaces"—the northerners who voted with the South—but they were motivated by other considerations. Senators Ninian Edwards and Jesse B. Thomas of Illinois, for example, voted with the South because they were themselves southerners and slaveholders. Henry Baldwin of Pennsylvania voted with the South in the hope of softening southern opposition to a higher tariff. Apparently several doughfaces agreed with the southern argument that imposing slavery restrictions on an incoming state would be unconstitutional. And apparently some northern Republicans were governed, like Jefferson, by deep suspicion of Federalist motives.

But what "perhaps did more than anything else to undermine Northern solidarity," says Glover Moore, was the fear of disunion.[24] Charles Kinsey of New Jersey, one of the handful of antislavery congressmen who determined the outcome of the struggle by switching to the southern side, gave eloquent expression to that fear in a speech delivered just before the decisive vote in the House. "On the next step we take depends the fate of unborn millions," he warned. Disunion, he said, presented itself "in all the horrid, gloomy features of reality," and a northern victory in the confrontation would be "an inglorious triumph, gained at the hazard of the Union."[25]

Throughout the crisis there was certainly a good deal of

southern talk about disunion and civil war, much of it in the form of flowery prediction rather than plain threat. Thus Senator Freeman Walker of Georgia envisioned "a brother's sword crimsoned with a brother's blood." And Thomas W. Cobb, another Georgian, declared that antislavery leaders had "kindled a fire which all the waters of the ocean" could not put out, and which only "seas of blood" could extinguish.[26] Yet the Missouri crisis was not a secession crisis, though it might have become one in time. Even the Richmond *Enquirer*, in bitterly accepting passage of the Compromise, acknowledged that the Union had never been in serious danger.[27] "If there had been a civil war in 1819–1821," says Moore, "it would have been between the members of Congress, with the rest of the country looking on in amazement." Moore goes on to suggest that "the Union would almost certainly have broken up at some time in the 1820's if . . . there had been an absolute refusal to compromise."[28] Perhaps so, but such a refusal, as he himself concludes, was a "remote possibility." For the longer the crisis lasted, the harder it became to keep Missouri out of the Union; and a truly imminent danger of disunion would have put unbearable pressure for compromise on many northern Republicans. Southerners did nevertheless begin to learn in the Missouri crisis how effectively the threat of disunion could be used as a weapon of southern defense.

The Missouri crisis in fact had many meanings and lessons for the South—some readily understood and others only vaguely sensed but often becoming clearer in the light of later events. For instance, the sudden appearance of an antislavery majority in the House of Representatives dramatically confirmed the southern need to maintain sectional equality in the Senate, but only dimly at best did any southerners in 1820 perceive the advantages of reestablishing a bisectional two-party system in national politics. The complaint of some southern congressmen that public discussion of the "delicate" subject of slavery increased the danger of slave revolts took on new meaning in 1822 after exposure of the Denmark Vesey conspiracy. It was not until the middle decades of the century, however, that the Missouri struggle came to be regarded as the beginning of southern degradation at the hands of the North. Thus Eli S. Shorter of Alabama would look back in anger from the floor of the House of Representatives in 1858: "We remember the compromise of 1820. The brand of inferiority was then stamped deep on the brow of southern manhood and southern honor; and there it remained, a burning disgrace, till the Kansas-Nebraska bill wiped it out and restored us to our long lost rights."[29]

In its constitutional aspects, the congressional debate on Missouri lent reinforcement to the old Republican preference for strict construction. The Tallmadge amendment, by proposing the gradual abolition of slavery in a prospective state *after* its admission to statehood, offered a much greater constitutional threat to the security of slavery than the Wilmot Proviso of later years. For, if antislavery spokesmen were right in asserting that any one of several clauses in the Constitution (such as the clause guaranteeing each state a republican form of government) could be construed as authorizing congressional regulation of slavery in a *new* state, what constitutional barrier remained to prevent the same kind of interference in the *oldest* of the slaveholding states? The Missouri struggle therefore connected antislavery sentiment more closely to broad construction and nationalism than it had ever been connected before. After 1820, it became increasingly difficult for a defender of slavery to support the expansion of federal power. John C. Calhoun managed to do so for just a few more years.

The Missouri debates also drew many a southerner unwillingly into discussion of the moral aspects of the slavery problem. Only a few militants like Senator William Smith of South Carolina defended the institution openly and absolutely, thus ushering in the "positive good" phase of proslavery ideology. For the most part, southern members of Congress were still willing to say that slavery was an evil—a curse, a cancer. Moore accordingly views the Missouri controversy as marking the end of an age in which southern thought had been dominated by the liberalism of the Enlightenment.[30]

Yet, upon close scrutiny, southern acknowledgment of the wrongness of slavery was largely an empty gesture in 1820. It had no effect on the main line of southern argument, which held the institution to be indispensable and ineradicable. The conflict between southern rhetoric and southern conviction was strikingly revealed in a speech by Congressman Robert Reid of Georgia. Reid at one point declared that the day when black Americans were given equal rights as citizens would be "most glorious in its dawning." But then he immediately added that such a "dream of philanthropy" could never be fulfilled, and that any person who acted upon such "wild theories" would become a "destroyer of the human family."[31]

The votes of southern congressmen in the Missouri struggle spoke more clearly than many of their speeches. Those votes indicated that the South had already made the most important decision in the whole history of the slavery controversy—and made it with virtual unanimity. That is, the Slaveholding South by 1820 had rejected the possibility of gradual emancipation, even in a new part of the country where it would have been neither impractical nor dangerous. It was this southern commitment to the *permanence* of slavery, and not the mere presence of slavery in the land, that made sectional conflict irrepressible and disunion increasingly probable as the nineteenth century advanced.

2 The Wilmot Proviso and the Mid-Century Crisis

Robert Toombs of Georgia was no typical fire-eater, but he spoke at times in flaming words. On December 13, 1849, Toombs warned the House of Representatives: "If by your legislation you seek to drive us from the territories of California and New Mexico . . . thereby attempting to fix a national degradation upon half the States of this Confederacy, *I am for disunion.*" Six months later he returned to the same theme, declaring:

I stand upon the great principle that the South has right to an equal participation in the territories of the United States. . . . She will divide with you if you wish it, but the right to enter all or divide I shall never surrender. . . . Deprive us of this right and appropriate this common property to yourselves, it is then your government, not mine. Then I am its enemy, and I will then, if I can, bring my children and my constituents to the altar of liberty, and like Hamilcar I would swear them to eternal hostility to your foul domination. Give us our just rights, and we are ready, as ever heretofore, to stand by the Union . . . Refuse it, and for one, I will strike for *Independence.*[1]

The crisis of 1846–1850 was truly a secession crisis—the first in American history. It began with the introduction of the

Wilmot Proviso and was the only sectional crisis ever precipitated by an effort to prohibit slavery in federal territory. From the southern point of view, as Toombs so eloquently asserted in Congress, it was a struggle to secure *equality* and to avoid *degradation*. Those two words and their equivalents appear repeatedly in southern speeches and editorials of the period. Thus Albert Gallatin Brown of Mississippi declared that he preferred disunion to "social and sectional degradation." Abraham W. Venable of North Carolina opposed the Compromise of 1850 because he considered it "degrading to the South." John B. Lamar of Georgia spoke of being "degraded into inequality." And Jefferson Davis after the Civil War said that the principal cause of the conflict had been "the systematic and persistent struggle to deprive the Southern States of equality in the Union."[2]

Southern members of Congress had appealed frequently to the principle of equality during the Missouri controversy, but they were then talking primarily about constitutional equality among the sovereign states of the Union, especially as it related to proposals for discriminatory restrictions on slaveholding in the state of Missouri. Southerners at that time were obviously less concerned about sectional equality in the territories; otherwise, a majority of them would not have supported the 36° 30′ restriction.

What southern leaders were demanding by mid-century was equality between the North and the South viewed almost as sovereign entities—equality most particularly in legal access to the federal territories, but equality also in moral standing. The bitter yearning for a lost respectability was well expressed by John C. Calhoun when he declared: "I am a southern man and a slaveholder; a kind and a merciful one, I trust—and none the worse for being a slaveholder. . . . I would rather meet any extremity upon earth than give up one inch of our equality . . .

What, acknowledge inferiority! The surrender of life is nothing to sinking down into acknowledged inferiority."[3]

Historians for more than a century have pondered the sectional struggle over slavery in the territories, trying to explain how it came to be invested with an emotional intensity that seems far out of proportion to its practical significance. The sum of all their scholarship still does not tell us clearly why the antebellum generation pursued to its disastrous conclusion an argument that became increasingly abstruse and that in any case had largely been settled by the forces of nature.

Some writers have concluded that much of the northern opposition to the extension of slavery was animated by ulterior political and economic motives. Some have interpreted southern expansionism as a natural function of the dynamics of plantation agriculture, while others have emphasized southern determination to maintain a sectional balance in the Senate as a shield against congressional assaults on slavery. The territorial controversy has also been interpreted as a hastening descent into irrationality and as a symbolic conflict in which the real issue was the future of slavery itself. Certainly, it can be added that southerners came to regard the status of slavery in the territories as a measure of their success or failure in the struggle for equality.

"The right to enter all or divide I shall never surrender," Toombs declared in 1850. Those were the only two bases for sectional equality in the territories. Either federal territory must *all* be open equally to northerners and to southerners (with their slaves), or it must be divided into northern and southern spheres of influence. The first alternative, though equitable in theory, was proslavery in its practical effects. For territory settled by a mixture of slaveholders and nonslaveholders became, as a matter of legal necessity, a slaveholding territory; and until 1861, all slaveholding territories became slaveholding states.

In providing governments for the trans-Appalachian West, Congress followed the policy of division. It prohibited slavery north of the Ohio River by reenacting the antislavery clause of the Northwest Ordinance. And it expressly exempted territories south of the river from the same clause, thus authorizing slavery by implication without officially establishing it. In providing governments for the Louisiana Purchase, however, Congress adopted the other policy, ostensibly neutral but actually proslavery, of opening the entire region to slaveholders and nonslaveholders alike. Furthermore, in the organization of Louisiana Territory (which became Missouri Territory in 1812 and covered all of the Purchase except the state of Louisiana), the policy was achieved by omitting *all* reference to slavery, even the familiar exemption from restriction that had become the rule in the Old Southwest. This was the Jeffersonian silence, embracing in purest form the principle that would later be called "nonintervention." It prevailed in the Louisiana Purchase until 1820. Then an upsurge of antislavery sentiment forced a return to the dual system, with slavery forbidden north of 36° 30′ and nonintervention silently continued south of that line.

Nonintervention, because of its negative character, was really just the first half of a territorial policy. In practice, it led to popular sovereignty. That is, it left the question of slavery to be decided by the people settling a territory. They did so informally at first, simply by bringing or not bringing slaves with them, and then officially through the action of their territorial government. But since nonintervention was a policy applied only to southern territories (except in the Louisiana Purchase before 1820), the territorial decisions down until the late 1850s were invariably in favor of slavery. Thus, historically although not necessarily, nonintervention meant popular sovereignty, and popular sovereignty meant slavery.

The Missouri Compromise settled the issue of slavery in the territories for a generation. Many southerners looked back upon it with a strange ambivalence. The memory of the antislavery attack rankled; the 36° 30' restriction embodied a demeaning and dangerous acknowledgment of congressional power. But at the same time, the concept of a dividing-line between free and slave territory carried an implication of sectional equality that never entirely lost its appeal in some southern eyes. Furthermore, as time passed, southerners tended increasingly to view the Compromise as an extraconstitutional settlement negotiated like a treaty between North and South in order to save the Union. As such, it implicitly exemplified Calhoun's principle of government by a concurrent majority.

The interval between the admission of Missouri and the introduction of the Wilmot Proviso was twenty-five years, almost to the day.[4] During those years, certain events and trends were shaping the crisis that David Wilmot precipitated on a sultry summer evening in 1846. In population, wealth, and industrial capacity, the South had fallen far behind the North and was much more conscious of its minority status than it had been a quarter of a century earlier. Yet, in the realm of politics, slaveholders were still the dominant social element in the government of the Republic.

The northern advantage in the House of Representatives had become greater than ever, it is true, but in the Senate there continued to be sectional parity. In fact, during the twenty-five years following the Missouri Compromise, three slave states and just one free state were admitted to the Union, and so on the day that Wilmot introduced his controversial Proviso, there were thirty southern senators and only twenty-six northern ones. The admission of Iowa later in 1846 and Wisconsin in 1848 restored the equilibrium.

Even more important to the South than its equal status in the Senate was the emergence of the second American party system. The bisectional strength of Whigs as well as Democrats meant that both parties had good reason to discountenance agitation of the slavery issue. Moreover, the Jacksonian Democrats—the stronger party of the two—were in many respects a resurrection of the Jeffersonian Republican organization that had served the South so well in its time. As the years passed, southern power and security came to depend more and more on southern dominance of the Democratic party.

Certainly the South in 1846 had many reasons to be pleased with its influence in national politics. The presidency continued to be in friendly hands. Southerners were still in the majority on the Supreme Court. Efforts to revive the national bank had failed, and tariff rates had been steadily reduced ever since the nullification crisis of 1832–1833.

Meanwhile, however, a new and uncommonly vehement challenge to southern security had emerged in the form of radical abolitionism, as personified by William Lloyd Garrison. There was a time when many historians regarded Garrison's launching of *The Liberator* on New Year's Day, 1831, as the opening gun of the Civil War. Albert J. Beveridge, working away on his biography of Lincoln in the 1920s, concluded that emancipation would have begun soon in the Border South had it not been for the Garrisonian crusade. "Darn those abolitionists," he wrote to Charles A. Beard. "The deeper I get into this thing, the clearer it becomes to me that the whole wretched mess could have been straightened out without the white race killing itself off, if the abolitionists had let matters alone."[5]

More recent scholarship has made it clear that the proslavery commitment of the South was well established before 1830 and therefore could not have originated as a response to the new antislavery radicalism. But if Garrisonian abolitionism was not the original cause of the sectional conflict over slavery, it nevertheless had a critical influence on the temper and shape of the conflict.

Out of passionate conviction, but also as a deliberate choice of strategy, the new abolitionists set out to destroy slavery by direct, personal attack upon everyone associated with the institution and everyone acquiescing in its existence. Their campaign of denunciation lacerated southern feelings as never before. The primary target, of course, was the slaveholder, whom they convicted of criminality, atrocity, and sin. Their language had the effect of degrading and dehumanizing the slaveholder, even as he was said to be degrading and dehumanizing his slaves.

The abolitionist crusade aggravated the southern fear that slave revolts could be inspired by northern agitation, and it evoked a related phenomenon of transcendent importance that perhaps can best be labeled "southern rage." By 1836, the crusade had turned Congress into a battleground over the receipt of abolitionist petitions and brought slavery to the center of national politics for the first time since the Missouri controversy.

To be sure, the abolitionists were highly unpopular in the North and constituted just a small fraction of the northern population. For the tactics of agitation, however, they were numerous enough to seem like an army, and their membership was heavily weighted with ministers, writers, editors, and other persons of more than average influence. Besides, the abolitionist movement was only part of a general antislavery trend that aroused apprehension and anger in the South. To understand fully the rage expressed by southerners like Robert Toombs during the crisis of 1846–1850, one must consider certain actions taken by northern state governments.

For example, Charles J. Faulkner of Virginia (later a congressman and minister to France) wrote to Calhoun in the summer of 1847 denouncing a piece of legislation as "the most deliberate and perfidious violation of all the guaranties of the

Constitution which the fanaticism and wickedness of the abolitionists have resorted to, and the most serious and dangerous attack yet made on the institution of slavery." Faulkner was talking, not about the Wilmot Proviso, as one might think, but rather about the personal liberty law recently enacted by the legislature of Pennsylvania. This measure, like others passed by northern states in the 1840s, was designed to protect free blacks from kidnapping, but it also impeded legitimate recovery of fugitive slaves. In addition, the new Pennsylvania law repealed a sojourning privilege dating back to 1788, whereby southerners could bring slaves into the state for visits of up to six months. Faulkner called the legislation of 1847 "a deliberate insult to the whole Southern people," which, among nations wholly independent, would be "a just cause for war." "Since the passage of this law," he wrote, "slaves are absconding from Maryland and this portion of Virginia in gangs of tens and twenties, and the moment they reach the Pennsylvania line all hopes of their recapture are abandoned."[6]

In respect to fugitive slaves, the South demanded not equality but special privilege of extraordinary proportions. Aside from the protection expected from the federal government, there was the right of private recapture, asserted and outlined by James M. Mason of Virginia on the Senate floor in January 1850. Under the fugitive-slave clause of the Constitution, said Mason, a slaveholder pursuing a fugitive into a free state had the right to enter any house without a warrant and seize an alleged slave by whatever force might be necessary. No person had a right to interfere with him or even to raise a question about the validity of his claim or the accuracy of his identification.[7] Thus the special privilege of the slaveholder took precedence over state sovereignty and civil liberty, even to the point of legalizing kidnapping. The fugitive-slave acts of 1793 and 1850 were both plainly unconstitutional if free Negroes came within the protection of the Fifth Amendment. There, indeed, was the essence of the dilemma. No law for the recovery of fugitive slaves could be effective without being outrageous. Yet southerners firmly believed that their right to an effective system of recovery was an article of solemn compact without which there could have been no Federal Union.

It appears that the number of slaves escaping into free states was relatively small—perhaps no more than a few hundred per year on the average. For southerners, however, the numbers were less important than the northern attitude and what it signified. "The loss of property is felt; the loss of honor is felt still more," Mason declared on a later occasion. "I say my people are degraded and humiliated when they are conscious that they tolerate a Government which is incapable of protecting them."[8] And when William H. Seward, during the debates of 1850, proposed a substitute bill guaranteeing accused fugitives the rights of habeas corpus and jury trial, there was this prompt and indignant response from Senator Henry S. Foote of Mississippi: "It cannot be that the American people have yet reached a depth of degradation so profound . . . as not to look upon this . . . attempt of the honorable Senator from New York to spoliate upon the . . . rights and interests of all the southern states . . . with pointed disapprobation, with hot contempt, with unmitigated loathing, and abhorrence unutterable."[9]

But the intensity of southern feeling on the subject is perhaps best indicated by the fact that the South Carolina Declaration of Causes of Secession, issued in December 1860, devoted twenty times as much space to the fugitive-slave problem as it did to the territorial question.[10]

Of course, the historical development most directly related to the crisis of 1846–1850 was the resumption of American territorial expansion after it had been in abeyance for a quarter of a century. The prospect of further expansion first arose in 1836 when the newly independent slaveholding Republic of Texas requested annexation to the United States. Fierce antislavery opposition greeted the proposal and helped delay annexation for nearly a decade. The Texas issue thus brought a militant antislavery movement into conflict with the new spirit of Manifest Destiny, exemplified in spread-eagle oratory and in wagons rolling westward to Oregon and California.

More than that, the Texas issue brought an enthusiastic expansionist named James K. Polk unexpectedly to the presidency and drove the United States predictably into hostilities with Mexico. Polk may or may not have been primarily responsible for starting the war, but he was certainly responsible for determining the *kind* of war it should be. His prompt dispatch of General Stephen W. Kearny to Santa Fe and Los Angeles indicated plainly enough that a war of territorial conquest had been set in motion. And so, just eight weeks after the declaration of war, David Wilmot introduced his famous Proviso.

The Wilmot Proviso was no fire bell in the night. It had been preceded by a decade of bitter sectional controversy in Congress over abolitionist petitions, slavery in the District of Columbia, and the annexation of Texas. The Proviso was sponsored, not by the most radical antislavery elements in Congress, but rather by a group of northern Democrats who had grown dissatisfied with southern domination of their party and with certain policies resulting from that domination. Some, for example, were angry about the recent presidential veto of a rivers-and-harbors appropriation, and some resented the Oregon Treaty signed with Great Britain in June. In each of these cases, the heavy hand of southern influence seemed all too visible. Polk's hostility to internal improvements at federal expense reflected the strict constructionism so dear to the Old South. As for Oregon, nearly half of it had been relinquished after the great expanse of Texas had been secured for slaveholders, and now southerners presumably expected to obtain still more slave territory as a prize of war. The Proviso, in the circumstances, seemed an appropriate retaliation. It forbade slavery in any territory that might be acquired from Mexico.

Here was a proposal so radical that it had no real precedent except perhaps Jefferson's abortive effort in 1784 to prohibit slavery throughout the trans-Appalachian West. Its full import did not become clear until the Treaty of Guadalupe Hidalgo in 1848 confirmed the cession of the Southwest to the United States. The Proviso, taken together with the general assumption that Oregon was bound to be free territory, would mean the exclusion of slavery from the entire American Far West, an area as large as the Louisiana Purchase. Compounding the outrageousness of the proposal, in southern eyes, was the fact that the land conquered from Mexico had cost lives as well as money. It had been purchased, the phrase ran, "by the blood and treasure" of the whole nation; yet half the nation was to be excluded from its benefits.

The Proviso itself would not have shocked the South and precipitated a sectional crisis if it had not received such overwhelming northern support in Congress and so much vehement endorsement in northern editorials, northern legislative resolutions, and northern party conventions. "The madmen of the North," said the Richmond *Enquirer*, ". . . have, we fear, cast the die, and numbered the days of this glorious Union." [11] The view that the southern states must secede if the Proviso should be enacted was probably more widespread in the South than the view in 1860 that the election of Lincoln would make secession necessary. Even Alexander H. Stephens said so. "The day in which aggression is consummated upon any section of the country . . . this Union is dissolved," he declared. "I would rather that the southern country should perish—that all her statesmen and all her gallant spirits should be buried in honorable graves—than submit for one instant to degradation." [12]

But the Proviso, although approved a number of times in the House of Representatives, never really had a chance of passing the Senate. Because of the nature of the crisis—because the crisis had been created in Congress and could be dissolved in Congress—the course of events was running through much passionate oratory toward another sectional compromise.

The struggle over the Wilmot Proviso resembled the Missouri controversy in a number of ways, but there were also some important differences between them. For one thing, the primary issue in 1819–1820 had been the admission of a slave state (Missouri), with the territorial question remaining secondary; whereas, in 1846–1850, the primary issue from the beginning was slavery in the territories, with admission of a free state (California) arising as a related but secondary matter.

As a consequence, the lines of argument were considerably different in the crisis of 1846–1850. For instance, the South, in order to defend its rights in the territories while adhering faithfully to the doctrine of state sovereignty, had to rely heavily upon what Arthur Bestor calls the principle of "extrajurisdictional" power—which meant, in effect, that a slaveholder entering federal territory, like a slaveholder pursuing a fugitive slave into another state, took with him the law of his own state and its protective force.[13]

Another difference between the two crises was that slavery had been legal under the preceding regime in Louisiana but illegal under the preceding regime in the Mexican Cession. Antislavery spokesmen could therefore argue that the equivalent of the Wilmot Proviso had been inherited from Mexico and would remain in force until superseded by American law. The argument, if valid, converted nonintervention, which had always been functionally permissive of slavery, into silent confirmation of a ban on slavery in the Southwest.

In response to this challenge, southerners elaborated and perfected the "common-property" doctrine—usually associated with resolutions introduced by Calhoun in 1847, although it had come into use some time before. Congress, according to the

Calhoun theory, was merely the "joint-agent" of the sovereign states and, as such, had no power to prevent the citizens of any states from "emigrating with their property" (meaning slaves) into the territories, which were not the property of the federal government, but rather the "common property" of the states. Slaveholding in the territories was therefore a right protected by the *direct force* of the Constitution, which superseded Mexican law in the Southwest and at the same time prevented Congress from enacting any such measure as the Wilmot Proviso.[14]

But of course the Constitution *has* no force until it is applied by some agency, and so the common-property doctrine, however appropriate it might be as an *answer* to the Proviso, was not a functional *alternative* to the Proviso. It was a theory of right and power but not a design of public policy. As a matter of policy, many southerners who embraced the common-property doctrine were prepared to advocate, or at least to accept, extension of the Missouri Compromise line to the Pacific. This involved them in the glaring inconsistency of denying the power of Congress to enact the Wilmot Proviso while acknowledging that same power if it were exercised only north of 36° 30′. Their explanation was that, in order to save the Union, they were willing to go beyond the restraints of the Constitution, though not beyond the principles of justice.

Extension of the Missouri Compromise line soon proved to be useless as a basis for compromise, however. Early in 1847, an effort to attach it by implication to a bill organizing Oregon Territory failed in the House of Representatives, 82 to 113, with only six northerners voting in the affirmative. Another such attempt the following year was defeated even more decisively, and Oregon, after two years of waiting, was finally organized as a free territory without reference to the rest of the Far West.[15]

Thus, a striking reversal had taken place. In 1820, the Missouri Compromise line had been a concession made to the

North as part of the price for the admission of Missouri as a slave state, and nearly half of the southern representatives had opposed it. In 1846–1847, extension of the line was demanded by southerners as the price for organization of Oregon as a free territory, and nearly all of the northern representatives opposed it. One reason for the change, as southerners resentfully noted, was that much more of the land at stake in 1846 lay south of 36° 30'.

As it became increasingly plain that extension of the 36° 30' line would never win acceptance, opponents of the Wilmot Proviso began to look for a more acceptable formula of compromise. One measure, sponsored unsuccessfully by John M. Clayton of Delaware in 1848, would have left the status of slavery in the Mexican Cession to judicial determination. Later that year, Stephen A. Douglas proposed that Congress admit the entire Southwest directly to statehood, thus bypassing the territorial stage and avoiding the convulsive territorial issue.[16]

Most important of all, however, was the solution brought forward by several northern Democrats and given the name "popular sovereignty." Congress, they maintained, could not, or at least should not, interfere with slavery in the territories and instead must leave the problem entirely to the decision of the territorial population. This doctrine, though offered as new theory, in fact recapitulated old practice. It described the policy established by Congress in 1790 for territory south of the Ohio River and reaffirmed in 1820 for that part of the Louisiana Purchase lying south of 36° 30'. Southerners in those earlier years of the Republic had not needed or asked for anything more— had not demanded positive federal laws protecting slavery in southern territories. But patterns of migration were changing in the 1840s, and the old policy of nonintervention could no longer be regarded as safely proslavery in its effect. Besides, the advocates of popular sovereignty like Douglas and Lewis Cass, in trying to sell the doctrine to their northern constituencies, laid heavy emphasis upon the power of territorial governments to prohibit slavery. And sometimes they added in stage whispers that, since nature had made the Southwest inhospitable to slavery, popular sovereignty would have the same effect there as the Wilmot Proviso, without giving mortal offense to the South.

Such argument did not encourage southern support, and the South, in fact, never developed much enthusiasm for the Cass-Douglas version of popular sovereignty. Yet, certain ambiguities in the doctrine made it useful to the Democratic party as a means of moderating and concealing internal sectional quarrels over slavery, especially in presidential election years. Northern Democrats and southern Democrats could talk about popular sovereignty (or nonintervention) and have different things in mind. This dissimulation was a frail vessel of party unity, but it stayed afloat until 1857, when the Supreme Court blew it out of the water.

When the Thirty-first Congress convened in December 1849, nearly two years after the Treaty of Guadalupe Hidalgo, the newly acquired Southwest was still without territorial organization, and the sectional crisis had reached its peak. The Gold Rush made California's need for stable government more urgent every day. The extravagant boundary claims of Texas seemed likely to produce violence in the Santa Fe region. Nearly all northern legislatures had passed resolutions endorsing the principle of the Wilmot Proviso. And southerners were becoming more and more convinced that in Zachary Taylor the nation had elected a reverse doughface—that is, a southern man with northern principles—to the presidency.

Taylor, who had fallen under the antislavery influence of William H. Seward and had said publicly that there would be no further extension of slavery, adopted as administration policy the old Douglas scheme of bypassing the territorial issue by admitting California and New Mexico directly to statehood.

Californians, with presidential encouragement but no authorization from Congress, proceeded to draft a constitution, establish a state government, and ask for admission to the Union as a free state.

The purpose of the Wilmot Proviso was about to be achieved by indirection, or so it appeared to outraged southerners. Any men of the South who would "consent to be thus degraded and enslaved," said Thomas L. Clingman of North Carolina, "ought to be whipped through their fields by their own negroes."[17] And Alexander H. Stephens, determined to resist "the dictation of Northern hordes of Goths and Vandals," suggested that southern states should be "making the necessary preparations of men and money, arms and munitions, etc., to meet the emergency."[18] The sense of emergency strengthened the movement toward southern unity, which culminated in an ominous call from Mississippi for a convention to meet in Nashville on the first Monday in June 1850. Our retrospective knowledge of what happened in 1850—especially Taylor's death and how it cleared the way for compromise—makes it extremely difficult for us to understand how desperate the situation seemed in the winter of 1849–1850.

Achievement of the Compromise of 1850 is one of the greatest legislative and oratorical events in American history, complete with moments of high drama, such as Calhoun's brooding valedictory presented just twenty-seven days before his death. The central issue was whether California should be admitted as a free state *with* or *without* accompanying concessions to the South in the rest of the Mexican Cession. But there were other problems also requiring attention, and Henry Clay provided a formula of general compromise in a set of resolutions introduced in the Senate on January 29.[19]

From that beginning, the familiar story line runs through the creation of a select Committee of Thirteen in April; the construction of the famous "Omnibus Bill" in May; Taylor's death and the destruction of the Omnibus in July; and then, between July 31 and September 17, passage of the Compromise as six separate measures in the Senate and five in the House of Representatives (where two bills were joined together for strategic reasons). The Compromise included the admission of California, organization of Utah and New Mexico territories without restrictions on slavery, reduction of the area of Texas, federal assumption of the Texas debt, prohibition of the domestic slave trade in the District of Columbia, and a more stringent fugitive-slave law.

All of the measures passed easily in the Senate. There was more resistance, as expected, at the other end of the Capitol. But the House, like its counterpart of thirty years earlier, ended by retreating from the position that it had held for so long and with such tenacity. In yielding to the strong pressure for compromise that had been built up during the many months of senatorial debate, the House not only surrendered the Proviso principle twice but also passed the provocative Fugitive Slave Act by a comfortable margin. All in all, it was a remarkable collapse of antislavery strength.

Only four senators and twenty-eight representatives voted for *all* the compromise measures. This is probably too strict a criterion to be useful, however; for a good many true supporters of compromise (like Douglas and Thomas Hart Benton) missed one or more of the final votes. If we define a supporter of the Compromise as someone who voted for at least four of the five measures related to the slavery question, and who opposed none of the five, the totals rise to fourteen in the Senate and forty-seven in the House. Of these sixty-one compromisers (constituting about 21 percent of the entire congressional membership), thirty-eight were northern Democrats, and eleven were southern Whigs—the two political groups that suffered most severely from the strains of party and sectional cross-pressures.[20]

Fifty-seven of the sixty-one, including thirteen from the Border South, represented states that did not leave the Union in 1860–1861. The eleven states of the Confederate South, whose total representation exceeded ninety, contributed only four compromisers, and there were none at all from South Carolina, Mississippi, Florida, Alabama, Georgia, and Louisiana—the first six states to secede in 1860–1861. Remember, if you will, how different it had been in 1820, when *northern* members of Congress were the ones overwhelmingly against the Compromise and the Lower South was relatively amenable to it.

In 1820, southerners had been forced to pay for the admission of Missouri as the only slave state extending north of the fortieth parallel. The payment was *prohibition* of slavery in the rest of the Louisiana Purchase lying north of 36° 30′. In 1850, northerners were made to pay for the admission of California as the first free state to extend south of the thirty-seventh parallel. The payment was *permission* of slavery in the rest of the Far West lying south of 42°.

If our conception of the Compromise of 1850 is expanded, as it should be, to include the organization of Oregon Territory in 1848 with slavery forbidden, it then becomes plain that the old policy of having two policies was continued. Unable to secure the extension of the Missouri Compromise line to the Pacific, the South, in effect, traded off the loss of southern California for the opening of Utah to slavery. As a consequence, the dividing-line, which had been first the Ohio River and then 36° 30′ (except for Missouri), became 42° in the Far West (except for California). North of the 42° dividing-line, slavery was prohibited in federal territory; south of the line, slavery was permitted in federal territory, just as had been the case ever since 1790. Stephens understood all of this very well. Replying to a critic back in Georgia who complained that he should have continued to support 36° 30′, he asked:

Do you mean the extension of the provisions of the Missouri Compromise, by which slavery was forever prohibited *north* of that line, leaving the people *south* of it to do as they pleased upon the subject of slavery? If so, was it not much better for the.South . . . to let the people do as they pleased over the whole territory up to 42 deg. north latitude, just as the Utah and New Mexican bills, which passed, provide, than to have the people *restricted* in any portion of the territory?[21]

Yet, for many Americans, 36° 30' had come to have a magical quality, and they regarded any policy without it as an abandonment of the entire dividing-line principle. Douglas, who spoke erroneously of 36° 30' as a dividing-line between freedom and *slavery*, seems never to have perceived that the territorial legislation of 1848–1850 continued a policy of dividing the West between freedom and *nonintervention*. Viewing the Utah and New Mexico acts without reference to Oregon, he saw them as introducing a new compromise principle—popular sovereignty—to replace the dividing-line policy. This misconception, with which he rationalized his sponsorship of the Kansas-Nebraska bill in 1854, has been perpetuated by a number of historians, most notably, perhaps, by Robert R. Russel in an influential article entitled "What Was the Compromise of 1850?"[22]

The Utah and New Mexico legislation did not constitute a compromise in itself, with "mutual concessions," as Russel maintains, and it did not install the Cass-Douglas version of popular sovereignty as official policy. Rather, the legislation constituted a victory for the South, offsetting the admission of California; for it rejected the Wilmot Proviso and embodied the principle of nonintervention, from which the Calhoun property-rights doctrine could be inferred, just as well as popular sovereignty. Russel concludes that it would be "futile to attempt to say which side came off the better" in the territorial legislation of 1850, but the members of Congress seem to have made the judgment readily enough. Eighty-two percent of the southerners in both houses voted for the Utah bill, and 62 percent of the northerners voted against it.

To have defeated the Proviso and secured passage of the first fugitive-slave law in over fifty years was no mean achievement for southern statesmanship. Acquiescence in the Compromise accordingly prevailed throughout the South, but not without a hard struggle in some states. The eventual triumph of Unionism everywhere is perhaps less significant than the fact that a sizable part of the electorate in South Carolina, Georgia, Alabama, and Mississippi continued to lean toward disunion even after the Compromise had been passed.[23]

Moreover, the Unionism that triumphed in the Lower South and Middle South was predominantly "conditional" Unionism —which is to say, conditional *dis*unionism. For, phrased either way, the concept meant: Under some conditions we will remain in the Union, and under other conditions we will not. The view of secession as a legal right probably gained considerable ground during the crisis. Howell Cobb, fighting Georgia secessionists in his famous campaign for governor in 1851, was one of those "Unionists" who found it wise to straddle the issue. The Federal Union was intended by its founders to be perpetual, he declared, and a state had no constitutional right to secede—except for just cause, to be determined by the state herself.[24]

Just as the Slaveholding South by 1820 had committed itself to the permanency of slavery, even while continuing to label the institution an evil, so the Confederate South by 1850 had embraced the principle of secessionism, even while rejecting immediate secession.[25] The Compromise legislation of 1850, though apparently resolving a number of vexatious and even dangerous problems, had scarcely touched the deeper, ineluctable conflict over slavery. The effect was to defuse the accumulated charge of sectional hostility without dismantling it. After so many stormy months of crisis, nearly everyone welcomed the period of relative calm that followed; but it was, in the words of one southern editor, "the calm of preparation, and not of peace."[26]

3 Kansas, Republicanism, and the Crisis of the Union

"All Christendom is leagued against the South upon this question of domestic slavery," said James Buchanan on the Senate floor in 1842. "They have no other allies to sustain their constitutional rights, except the Democracy of the North. . . . In my own State, we inscribe upon our banners hostility to abolition. It is there one of the cardinal principles of the Democratic party."[1]

The crisis of 1850 once again confirmed the crucial importance of northern Democrats in the southern strategy of defense, and it also revealed the extent to which that defense might be breached by an unsympathetic president. The South accordingly appears to have benefited more from the political consequences of the Compromise of 1850 than from any of its specific provisions. For a reunited Democratic party, pledging faithful adherence to the Compromise, swept to victory in the presidential election of 1852 and also won a two-thirds majority in the House of Representatives.

During the next eight years, under Franklin Pierce and his successor, James Buchanan, southern influence dominated the executive branch of the federal government through the agency of northern doughfaces like Caleb Cushing and Jeremiah S.

Black, as well as southerners like Jefferson Davis and Howell Cobb. Throughout the period, the Senate remained safely Democratic and therefore safely prosouthern on slavery questions. In the House of Representatives, three of the five speakers serving between 1850 and 1860 were Democrats from Georgia, Kentucky, and South Carolina. Seven of the nine members of the Supreme Court were Democrats; and in 1857, six of them declared the Missouri Compromise restriction unconstitutional on the ground that Congress had no power to prohibit slavery in the territories.

Of course, these were things that southerners had come to expect. In 1861, Alexander H. Stephens reminded his fellow Georgians: "We have had a majority of the Presidents chosen from the South; as well as the control and management of most of those chosen from the North." Then he went on to name other offices in which southerners had outnumbered northerners: Supreme Court justices, 18 to 11; speakers of the House, 23 to 12; presidents pro tem of the Senate, 24 to 11; attorneys general, 14 to 5; foreign ministers, 86 to 54; and in the appointment of some 3,000 clerks, auditors, and controllers, better than a two-to-one advantage.[2]

The extraordinary power traditionally exercised by southerners in national affairs constituted one of the principal deterrents to disunion; for as long as it endured, the South had better reason to remain in the Union than to leave. It was the loss of a substantial part of that power in 1860 that drove the seven states of the Lower South into secession, and the critical element in the loss was the weakened condition of the South's only ally in Christendom—the northern Democracy.

The structure of southern power in national politics during the 1850s was a kind of holding-company arrangement in which the South held majority control of the Democratic party, and the Democrats were the majority party in the nation. The same pattern had prevailed during much of the preceding half century, and the recent experience with Zachary Taylor had revealed that the Whig party could *not* be brought under southern control—not even when it was headed by a southern slaveholder. In any case, the distress of the Whig party soon left the Democrats as the only national party organization through which the South could exercise national power.

Nothing, then, was more vital to southern security within the Union than maintaining the majority status of the Democratic party. And in this respect, the Democratic victory in 1852 was not as overwhelming as it appeared on the surface, especially in the North. Although Pierce carried fourteen out of the sixteen free states, he did so with only a plurality of their popular vote. The structure of southern political power therefore resembled a bridge that rested at one end on an insecure foundation. To be sure, Democratic mastery seemed firm enough in 1853, with the presidency recaptured and the party controlling both houses of the incoming Congress by huge majorities. But this flush of prosperity proved to be ominous, in a way, and also treacherous —ominous because of what it signified about the condition of the Whig party, and treacherous because it encouraged the disastrous blunder of the Kansas-Nebraska Act.

The disintegration of the Whig party, and thus of the second American party system, began with the alienation of southern Whigs from Taylor in 1849–1850 and was largely completed by 1855. Historians continue to ponder the question of why the Whig party perished in the 1850s while the Democratic party, though presumably subject to the same disruptive pressures, managed to survive. It may be, simply, that the Whigs lacked the symbolic appeal, the tradition of victory, and the degree of cohesion necessary for survival in the 1850s. Another explanation is that Whiggery was in a sense absorbed by the burgeoning nativist movement, which then failed in *its* efforts to become a major, bisectional party. But in addition, it appears that differences of sectional balance *within* the two parties may account for the greater vulnerability of the Whigs. Since the South was much more united than the North on the issue of slavery, it was accordingly easier for many northern Democrats to remain within a party increasingly dominated by proslavery southerners than it was for southern Whigs to remain within a party increasingly dominated by antislavery northerners. That is probably why the disruption of the second American party system started with the collapse of Whiggery in several states of the Lower South.[3]

Why the Whig organization did not at least survive in the North as a major antislavery party, instead of giving way to the Republicans, is another question and need not be answered here.[4] The point is that the death of the Whig party as a national organization proved harmful to the health of the Democratic party and thus to the structure of southern political power. For the Democrats, during the later 1850s, were opposed in both the North and the South by sectional or local parties that did not have to make any concessions to intersectional accommodation within their organizations. The cross-pressures of party and section upon northern Democrats became much more severe when the Whigs were replaced by a more aggressively antislavery party that stood to profit organizationally from continued agitation of the slavery issue. The challenge of Republicanism compelled men like Stephen A. Douglas, in the interest of political survival, to show more independence of southern influence where slavery was concerned, and this necessity could not fail to place heavy strains upon party unity.

And even in the South, where the Democrats themselves were supposedly the radical party on sectional issues, they came under cross-pressure from the post-Whig opposition parties, which, as a matter of political strategy, often tried to outdo them in proslavery extremism. It was the southern opposition press, for instance, that started the attacks on Buchanan's Kansas policy in the summer of 1857, and it was the southern opposition press that set up the loudest clamor for a territorial slave code two years later. As John V. Mering has pointed out, "Only in Tennessee among southern states that had elections for governor in 1859 did the Opposition refrain from taking a stronger stand on behalf of slavery in the territories than the Democrats."[5]

But the first baneful consequence of the Whig decline was passage of the Kansas-Nebraska bill, which never could have been accomplished if the Democrats had not held such large majorities in both houses of Congress. The bill received the support of nearly nine-tenths of all southern members casting votes and nearly three-fourths of all Democrats. It was an official party measure, endorsed and vigorously promoted by the Pierce administration, but its disruptive influence is strikingly illustrated by the fact that in the House of Representatives, northern Democrats were divided, 44 in favor and 44 against.[6] The political aftermath turned into a Democratic nightmare, with waves of popular indignation sweeping through the free states, 66 out of 91 House seats held by northern Democrats lost in the midterm elections, and the emergence of a broad anti-Nebraska coalition that would soon crystallize into the Republican party.

The struggle over the Kansas-Nebraska bill was the most egregious of several instances in which southerners, during the 1850s, traded some of their power advantage for empty sectional victories. Although its momentous consequences are plain to see, the struggle is of interest not only because of what it did *to* the South, but also because of what it revealed *about* the South.

Historians differ about the degree to which southerners of the 1850s were committed to the further expansion of slavery. The South delineated by William L. Barney, for instance, was a society in constant need of more room for its growing slave population and of new land to replace its easily depleted soils. "The continual maturation of slavery within a fixed geographical area," he writes, "created class and racial stresses that could be relieved only through expansion." Furthermore, "as long as the option of adding slave territory was kept open, Southerners could delude themselves with the comforting belief that eventually slavery and its terrible racial dilemma could vanish slowly and painlessly, by a diffusion of all the blacks out of the American South into the tropics of Central and South America."[7]

On the other hand, there are historians disposed to believe that the sectional controversy of the 1850s had less to do with the further expansion of slavery than with the future of slavery in modern America. In their view, the pernicious and seemingly useless quarrel over the territories was primarily a symbolic struggle laden with implication—or, as has been said, "merely the skirmish line of a larger and more fundamental conflict."[8]

No doubt there is room enough for both interpretations in any comprehensive explanation of the coming of the Civil War, but southern expansionism hardly seems to have been the animating spirit of the Kansas-Nebraska Act. The measure, by repealing the 36° 30' restriction of the Missouri Compromise, admitted slavery into an area unsuited for it and in no way facilitated the expansion of slavery southward into areas that *were* suited for it.

It is true that some southerners cherished the hope of making Kansas the sixteenth slave state, but even if they had succeeded, it would have been a nominal and temporary triumph gained at excessive cost. Proslavery imperialism became an absurdity in Kansas, and, as far as southern political power was concerned, it would have been much better strategy to settle for the admission of Kansas as a free but *Democratic* state, like the three states actually admitted in the 1850s—California, Minnesota, and Oregon. That was precisely the strategy adopted by Robert J. Walker as governor of Kansas in 1857, but the South rose up in revolt against it and saw Kansas admitted just a few years later as a Republican state instead.

The bitterest irony in the Kansas-Nebraska Act was that its sponsors justified it as a logical and reconciliatory extension of the Compromise of 1850. They insisted, erroneously, that the old dividing-line policy had been replaced with a new, uniform national policy of nonintervention and that, accordingly, to retain the slavery restriction north of 36° 30' in the organization of new territories would violate the letter and spirit of the recent Compromise. Actually, however, the popularity of the Compromise of 1850 resulted largely from its general pacificatory effect, not from any principles that could be inferred from its specific provisions. In short, the clearest violation of the spirit of the Compromise would be *any* legislative action that revived the slavery controversy. And the political power of the South, depending as it did upon the strength and unity of the Democratic party, likewise stood to suffer grievously from any renewal of slavery agitation. Southerners must have realized as well as Douglas that repeal of the Missouri Compromise restriction would, in his words, "raise a hell of a storm." Why, then, did they risk so much for so little to be gained?

For one thing, it appears that the southern members of Congress more or less drifted into the Kansas-Nebraska struggle without giving it much thought beforehand. Certainly there was no strong pressure on them from home to secure the repeal at that time, and it is notable that members from the Lower South were not prominent in the early stages of the affair. In fact, the senator who initiated the move to make the repeal explicit was a Kentucky Whig—the successor of Henry Clay.

Southern press support for the Kansas-Nebraska bill was relatively restrained, as Avery O. Craven has shown. "It is difficult for us to comprehend, or credit the excitement . . . in the North on account of the Nebraska question," wrote an Alabaman in the summer of 1854. "Here," he continued, "there is no excitement, no fever, on the subject. It is seldom alluded to in private or public and so far as the introduction of slavery [into Kansas and Nebraska] is concerned, such a consummation is hardly hoped for."[9] But the savage northern denunciation of the measure encouraged southern members to close ranks on the issue, and they supplied more than 60 percent of the votes cast for passage. With sectional violence thereafter erupting and becoming chronic on the prairies of Kansas, the South's emotional investment in the proslavery cause in Kansas grew to enormous proportions, even while the chances of gaining anything of practical importance were steadily dwindling.

Southern attitudes throughout the Kansas controversy demonstrate the intensely reactive nature of southern sectionalism. That is, the South did not so much respond to the Kansas-Nebraska issue itself as react to the northern response to the issue; and much the same thing happened four years later in the struggle over the Lecompton constitution. Similarly, what angered southerners most about John Brown's raid on Harpers Ferry was the amount of applause it received in the North.

The language of antislavery denunciation had a cumulative effect by the 1850s, and southern skin, far from toughening under attack, had become increasingly sensitive. According to Senator Judah P. Benjamin of Louisiana, the heart of the matter was not so much what the abolitionists and Republicans had *done* or might *do* to the South, as it was "the things they *said*" about the South—and the moral arrogance with which they said them.[10] Southerners, though often emphatically denying it, in fact cared deeply about northern opinion of the South and its people. They wanted, above all, an end to being treated as moral inferiors, and thus an end to the fear of eventually *accepting* the badge of inferiority. The result, says Charles G. Sellers, was a "series of constantly mounting demands for symbolic acts by which the North would say that slavery was all right."[11]

The most conspicuous badge of sectional inferiority was overt federal prohibition of slavery in the territories. For many southerners by the 1850s, such exclusion had become a moral reproach of unbearable weight. When Douglas offered them the opportunity to erase a large part of the stigma by repealing the Missouri Compromise restriction, they could scarcely do otherwise than grasp it.

The symbolic victory thus achieved in the Kansas-Nebraska Act was not really expected to bring any tangible benefits. But the course of events in Kansas did conspire to offer the South a chance in 1858 to win another victory of the same kind—that is, the admission of Kansas as a nominal slaveholding state under the Lecompton constitution. Once again, and in an even more dubious cause, southern members of Congress closed ranks. Knowing that the constitution did not represent the will of the territorial population, knowing that Kansas was destined to be a free state whatever the formal terms of her admission might be, and knowing that the issue would surely cause havoc among the northern Democracy, they nevertheless voted almost unanimously for the Lecompton bill.[12]

Again there appeared to be an important principle at stake. For here was an opportunity to test one of the items in the Georgia platform of 1850—namely, whether a slave state could ever again be admitted to the Union, now that an antislavery party had become predominant in the North. There had *been* no such admission, after all, since that of Texas twelve years earlier. The test came, moreover, in the aftermath of the Dred Scott decision, when southerners were again reacting to a northern reaction and also discarding the notion that the Constitution, of its own force, gave them any protection against antislavery attack.

As it became increasingly clear that the Lecompton bill, with half of the northern Democrats opposing it, could not command a majority in the House, another secession crisis developed. The ultimatum "Lecompton or disunion" reverberated in the halls of Congress, in the southern press, and in southern legislatures. With Alabama leading the way, contingent steps toward secession were officially taken by several states. "Upon the action of this Congress, must depend the union or disunion of this great Confederacy," a Georgia congressman warned. The people of the South were determined, he said, "to have equality in this Union or independence out of it . . . you must admit Kansas . . . with the Lecompton constitution."[13] "The equilibrium in the balance of power is already lost," declared a member from Mississippi. "Reject Kansas and the cordon is then completed. . . . Against this final act of degradation I believe the South will resist—resist with arms."[14] "Save the Union, if you can," wrote a South Carolinian to Senator James H. Hammond. "But rather than have Kansas refused admission under the Lecompton Constitution, let it perish in blood and fire."[15]

The symbolic importance of the issue was not diminished but rather was enhanced by the fact that the South had nothing material to gain from the admission. As Buchanan's pro-Lecompton message to Congress perceptively argued: "In considering this question, it should never be forgotten that in proportion to its insignificance . . . the rejection of the constitution will be so much the more keenly felt by the people of . . . the States of this Union, where slavery is recognized."[16] So, paradoxically, the very futility of the proslavery cause in Kansas made the Lecompton question more clearly a "point of honor" and a meaningful test of how *little* could be expected from the North in the way of concessions. In the words of one South Carolinian, it would have been "dirt cheap" for the free states to yield.[17]

Once again, however, a legislative crisis ended in a legislative compromise—or rather, in this case, a pseudocompromise that did not conceal the reality of southern defeat. The critical question was whether the Lecompton bill should be passed as it was or be amended to allow resubmission of the constitution to the voters of Kansas, which would surely mean rejection. With the House of Representatives this time standing its ground, southern members of Congress ended by accepting the so-called "English compromise," which provided for an indirect resubmission of the constitution and thus allowed them to save face a little with their constituents.

For this miserable achievement the South paid dearly. The Democratic party, split by an anti-Lecompton revolt with Douglas at its head, suffered another election defeat in 1858 and became the minority party in virtually every northern state. From that point on, the odds favored election of a Republican president in 1860. Moreover, the English compromise was so obviously a southern backdown from the threat of disunion that it encouraged Republicans to regard later secession threats as mere resumption of a game of bluff.

The compromise nevertheless satisfied many southerners, even some aiming at disunion, because it enabled them to retreat from a shaky limb. The Lecompton constitution, for a number of reasons, provided a very dubious basis for a sectional ultimatum. Governor Joseph E. Brown of Georgia, who was ready at the time to inaugurate a secession movement, later acknowledged that an outright defeat of the Lecompton bill would have caused "great confusion," and that "the democratic party of the state would have been divided and distracted."[18] It appears, then, that in 1858 there was some possibility of an *unsuccessful* secession movement that might have thrown secessionism generally into disrepute and thus, like a small earthquake, taken off some of the underlying stress.

The Lecompton affair proved to be the last full-dress legislative crisis and compromise in the tradition of 1819–1821, 1832–1833, and 1846–1850. Reflecting upon the pattern of events from the introduction of the Tallmadge proviso to the hollow triumph of the English compromise, one is disposed to doubt that legislative crisis was ever the proper fuse for setting off a civil war in the United States. A crisis arising in Congress could usually be controlled by Congress. The greatest danger in 1850, for instance, had been that presidential intervention might take matters out of congressional hands.

The end of the Lecompton controversy in fact marked the end of the territorial issue as a serious threat to the Union. Kansas ceased to be disputed ground and was admitted quietly as a free state in 1861. There was no other sectional issue with which Congress seemed likely, in the near future, to create another legislative crisis. Certainly not the agitation for a reopening of the African slave trade; for that had only minority support even in the Lower South. And certainly not the issue of a slave code for the territories, which provoked so much congressional debate in 1859 and 1860. That was not a southern demand upon Congress for legislation, but rather a southern Democratic demand upon Douglas for renunciation of his apostasy or withdrawal from the approaching presidential race.

James Buchanan had entered the presidency in 1857 determined to end the conflict in Kansas and thereby restore sectional peace. He hoped that "geographical parties," as he phrased it in his inaugural, would then "speedily become extinct."[19] His efforts ended in a curious mixture of success and failure; for the resolution of the Kansas problem, by the very manner in which it was accomplished, substantially increased the strength of the Republican party.

The disintegration of the Whig party, and hence the breakup of the second American party system, had begun before 1854, but it was the Kansas-Nebraska Act, more than anything else, that determined the character of the third party system in its early years. If the sectional truce of 1850 had remained more or less in effect, the Whig party might well have been succeeded by the Native American or Know-Nothing party. Instead, with the slavery controversy reopened to the point of violence, the anti-

Nebraska coalition of 1854 swiftly converted itself into the nation's first major party organized on antislavery principles. Suddenly, the South faced a new menace and a new potential cause for secession—the possibility that a Republican might be elected to the presidency.

The causes for secession listed in the Georgia platform of 1850, it will be remembered, had all been legislative acts that might be passed by Congress.[20] The sectional crises of 1820, 1833, 1850, and 1858 had all been precipitated by such legislation, enacted or proposed. But, beginning in 1856, the election of a Republican president became a more probable occasion for disunion than any legislative proposal likely to receive serious consideration in Congress. Beginning in 1856, a different finger was on the trigger mechanism. Control passed from the professional politician to the ordinary voter, particularly the northern voter. And if worse should come to worst, how did one go about compromising the results of a presidential election?

It was difficult for the people of the South to view Republicans as merely a political opposition. "If they should succeed in this contest," said a North Carolina newspaper in September 1856, "the result will be a separation of the States. No human power can prevent it. . . . They would create insurrection and servile war in the South—they would put the torch to our dwellings and the knife to our throats. They are, therefore, our enemies."[21]

We should perhaps pay more attention to the fact that 1856 was a year of genuine secession crisis, mitigated only by the general belief that the Republicans had but an outside chance of capturing the presidency. For southerners, the outcome of the election spelled temporary relief but very little reassurance. The Democrats did elect James Buchanan to succeed Franklin Pierce, and they did recapture control of the House of Representatives. Buchanan triumphed by sweeping the South, except for Maryland, and by carrying also the five free states of New Jersey, Pennsylvania, Indiana, Illinois, and California. But only two of those five states gave him popular majorities—Indiana, 50.4 percent, and his own Pennsylvania, 50.1 percent. The Democratic share of the free-state vote fell from 50.7 percent in 1852 to 41.4 percent in 1856. John C. Frémont, the Republican candidate, outpolled Buchanan in the North by more than a hundred thousand votes. Frémont and Millard Fillmore, the American party candidate, together outpolled him by more than a half million votes in the North. There was little difficulty visualizing what would happen to the Democratic party in the free states if its divided opposition should become united. The party had, in fact, hung on to the presidency with its fingertips; and the loss of that precarious hold, even many conservative southerners agreed, would mean a prompt disruption of the Union.

In these circumstances, the all-out drive to make Kansas a slave state under the Lecompton constitution was plain political folly. And the midterm congressional elections of 1858 accordingly proved disastrous for the Democrats because of what happened in those same northern states that Buchanan had carried two years earlier. The Republicans increased their share of the total vote in New Jersey, Pennsylvania, Indiana, and Illinois from 35 percent in 1856 to 52 percent in 1858. The most stunning reversal came in Pennsylvania. There, just the year before, the Democrats had elected a governor by more than forty thousand votes, but in 1858 they lost nearly all of their congressional seats and were outpolled by twenty-five thousand votes. "We have met the enemy in Pennsylvania," said Buchanan, "and we are theirs."[22]

From the Lecompton struggle onward, all the signs of the times pointed to a Republican victory in 1860 and to some kind of secession movement as a consequence. Yet the Democratic party, instead of reuniting to meet the danger, became increasingly a house divided against itself. The quarrel between Douglas and the South, aside from its strong influence on the shape of the final crisis, deserves attention because of what it reveals about the psychological escalation of the sectional conflict.

Douglas in 1856 had been the favorite presidential nominee of the South, and especially of the Lower South, which gave him thirty-eight of its forty-seven votes at the Cincinnati convention. Four years later at Charleston, however, delegates from the Lower South walked out of the convention rather than accept his leadership of the party. In the interval, Douglas made his fight against the Lecompton constitution, opposing even the English compromise; he issued the Freeport doctrine during the debates with Lincoln as a means of salvaging the principle of popular sovereignty while at the same time endorsing the Dred Scott decision; and, presumably as a consequence of those actions, he managed to win reelection to the Senate against the Republican tide that swept so many northern Democrats out of office in 1858.

It was success at the polls that the South needed most from its northern allies, but what southern Democratic leaders proceeded to insist upon instead was party orthodoxy, as they defined it. Ignoring the plain fact that for Douglas, opposition to the Lecompton constitution had been a matter, not only of principle, but also of political survival, they branded him a traitor. And ignoring the fact that the Freeport doctrine was actually of southern origin, they branded him a heretic. As punishment, the Senate Democratic leadership in December 1858 stripped him of his chairmanship of the committee on territories, a position that he had held continuously for more than ten years.[23]

Douglas responded with his usual vigor and combativeness. The southern Democrats, in turn, set out to make approval of a territorial slave code the supreme test of party loyalty. That was the ostensible issue that eventually disrupted the party at Charleston, but the real issue was Douglas, and the purpose of the slave-code agitation was to destroy him as a presidential candidate.

Of course, the South never approached unanimity in such matters, and the Little Giant continued to have supporters in every southern state right down to 1860. Even the Lower South gave him 11 percent of its total popular vote for president that year. One is nevertheless struck by the volume and intensity of southern hatred for Douglas in the period 1858–1860. He was with us, the indictment ran, "until the time of trial came; then he deceived and betrayed us." He "placed himself at the head of the Black column and gave the word of command," thereby becoming "stained with the dishonor of treachery without a parallel in the political history of the country." And now, covered with the "odium of . . . detestable heresies" and the "filth of his defiant recreancy," he would receive what southern patriots had always given northern enemies—"war to the knife." Then, "away with him to the tomb which he is digging for his political corpse."[24]

In retrospect, it appears that the only hope of preventing a Republican presidential victory lay in uniting the Democratic party behind Douglas. Yet, by 1860, southern hostility toward Douglas had taken on a life of its own and become implacable. The motives of southern leaders at this point are not easily fathomed or summarized. Perhaps as many as a score of them harbored serious presidential aspirations and so had personal reasons for wanting Douglas out of the way. There were also committed secessionists working openly to disrupt the Democratic party and welcoming the likelihood of a Republican presidential victory as the best means of achieving disunion. Covertly or subconsciously allied with them was a larger group of southerners (including Jefferson Davis, for example) who continued to call secession a "last resort," while conducting themselves in a way that tended to eliminate other choices. Their "conditional Unionism" with impossible conditions amounted to secessionism in the end.

But in addition to all the purposes visible in southern attitudes toward Douglas, his defection had an important symbolic meaning that weighed heavily on the southern spirit. The theme of betrayal and fear of betrayal runs prominently through much of the southern rhetoric of alienation. The South had been betrayed, in a sense, by its own ancestors who first accepted the role of slaveholder. It felt betrayed by New England, whose abolitionist zealots now made war on an institution introduced into the country by New England slave traders. It felt betrayed by Taylor as president and by Walker as territorial governor of Kansas. Southerners also feared treachery from their slaves and free blacks. They distrusted the sectional loyalty of nonslaveholding southern whites, and in the Lower South there was strong doubt that the border states could be depended upon in a crisis.

In such a context, the defection of Douglas was an especially painful blow. Perhaps no single event contributed so much to the southern sense of being isolated in a hostile world. "[It] has done more than all else," wrote a South Carolinian, "to shake my confidence in Northern men on the slavery issue, for I have long regarded him as one of our . . . most reliable friends." A correspondent of the Charleston *Mercury* put it more tersely: "If he proved false, whom can you trust?"[25] To despair of Douglas was virtually to despair of the Union itself. At the Charleston convention in the spring of 1860, the states of the Lower South withdrew from the Democratic party organization rather than submit to the nomination of Douglas. Who could then doubt that those same states would withdraw from the Union rather than submit to the election of a Republican president? In this respect, the dramatic walkout of delegates at Charleston was a dress rehearsal for secession.

The final crisis of the Union is commonly thought of as starting with the election of Lincoln in November 1860, but the entire presidential campaign had taken place in an atmosphere of crisis that extended back into the preceding year. When the Thirty-sixth Congress convened on December 5, 1859, John Brown was just three days in his grave, and the storm of emotion caused by his adventure at Harpers Ferry had not yet begun to abate. The House of Representatives plunged immediately into a two-month-long speakership contest of such bitterness that many members of Congress armed themselves for protection against assault. One senator, with grim hyperbole, said that the only persons not carrying a revolver and a knife were those carrying two revolvers.

Then, after an angry renewal of the slave-code debate in the Senate, there came the splitting of the Democratic party at Charleston. By midsummer, many southerners recognized that the odds strongly favored a Republican victory, and they began, in their minds, at least, to prepare for it. October elections for state offices in Pennsylvania and Indiana turned probability almost into certainty, and still there was another month left for preparation.

Meanwhile, with the apprehension aroused by John Brown still keenly felt, a new wave of fear swept through the South. There were reports of slaves in revolt, of conspiracies uncovered just in time, of mass poisonings attempted, of whole towns burned, and of abolitionist agents caught and hung. And the full terror, presumably, still lay ahead. "If such things come upon us," said a Georgia newspaper, "with only the *prospect* of an Abolition ruler, what will be our condition when he is *actually in power?*"[26] The very vagueness of the prospect made it all the more ominous. Fear of Republican rule was to no small degree a fear of the unknown. Chief Justice Roger B. Taney was not alone in believing that the news of Lincoln's election might be the signal for a general slave uprising. But other prophets of doom, like the editors of the Richmond *Enquirer*, pictured Republican purposes working out in more insidious ways:

> Upon the accession of Lincoln to power, we would apprehend no direct act of violence against negro property, but by the use of federal office, contracts, power and patronage, the building up in every Southern State of a Black Republican party, the ally and stipendiary of Northern fanaticism, to become in a few short years the open advocates of abolition. . . . No act of violence may ever be committed, no servile war waged, and yet the ruin and degradation of Virginia will be as fully and fatally accomplished, as though bloodshed and rapine ravished the land.[27]

One wonders how often in history rebellions and other cataclysmic events have not occurred, even in the presence of adequate causes, simply because there was no practical point of impulse where feeling and belief could be translated into action. For southerners, the presidential election of 1860 was just such a point of impulse—its date fixed on the calendar, its outcome predictable and not subject to compromise, its expected consequences vague but terrible. All the passion of the sectional conflict became concentrated, like the sun's rays by a magnifying glass, on one moment of decision that could come only once in history—that is, the *first* election of a Republican president. If secessionists had not seized the moment but instead had somehow been persuaded to let it pass, such a clear signal for action might never again have sounded.

Yet, even under these optimum conditions created by Lincoln's election, the southern will to act was but partly energized. The South, though long united in defense of slavery, had never been close to unity on the subject of secession. And so, in the end, the best fuse available set off only half of the accumulated charge. Just the seven states of the Lower South broke away from the Union in the winter of 1860–1861, although their very number, as I have already suggested, probably had a critical influence on the subsequent course of events.

But if only the Lower South seceded, the entire Slaveholding South had contributed heavily to the event that activated the secession movement—that is, to the Republican capture of the presidency. In 1852, the Free Soil candidate for president received only 7 percent of the popular vote in the free states and did not come close to winning a single electoral vote. Just eight years later, Lincoln won 55 percent of the popular vote in the free states and 98 percent of their electoral vote. It is difficult to believe that a political revolution of such magnitude would have occurred if southerners had not chosen to pursue the will-o'-the-wisp of Kansas, sacrificing the realities of power to an inner need for reassurance of their equal status and moral respectability in the face of antislavery censure.

The Charleston *Mercury*, commenting on the Dred Scott decision in 1857, said that it was "a victory more fatal, perhaps, than defeat," because the antislavery forces always rose up stronger after each sectional confrontation and, in fact, seemed to feed on adversity.[28] Pursuing the same theme more than a century later, David M. Potter wrote:

> For ten years the Union had witnessed a constant succession of crises; always these ended in some kind of "victory" for the South, each of which left the South with an empty prize and left the Union in a weaker condition than before. . . . Not one of [the victories] added anything to the area, the strength, the influence, or even the security of the southern system. Yet each had cost the South a high price, both in alienating the public opinion of the nation and in weakening . . . the Democratic party, which alone stood between the South and sectional domination by the Republicans.[29]

Yet the victories of the South, though useless, were not meaningless. Important values seemed to be at stake—values associated, above all, with regional and personal self-respect. More than one southern political leader insisted that the fight for the Lecompton constitution had to be made because it was a "point of honor." With the same sensitivity about honor and the same disregard for possible consequences, many a southerner had faced his opponent on the dueling ground.

In the spring of 1861, with secession accomplished and the Confederate States of America a functioning reality, there remained still another point of honor to be settled, another empty prize to be won at exorbitant cost. It appears now that the Confederacy's best hope of survival may have been to avoid war and consolidate its independent status as long as possible, rather than trying to win a war against a stronger enemy. But the stars and stripes still flying on a fortified island in Charleston Harbor had become an infuriating symbol of southern independence unrecognized and thus another instance of southern honor degraded. So, in the early morning of April 12, 1861, southerners once again did what they had to do. They opened fire on Fort Sumter and this time gained a military victory more disastrous, perhaps, than any of their later military defeats.

Appendix

The following summary of southern roll call votes in Congress is based (with one correction) upon tables in Glover Moore, *The Missouri Controversy, 1819–1821* (Lexington: University of Kentucky Press, 1966), pages 53, 55, 109, 111, and Holman Hamilton, *Prologue to Conflict: The Crisis and Compromise of 1850* (Lexington: University of Kentucky Press, 1964), pages 191–92, 195–200. In each instance, the affirmative vote is given first. The eight measures included are:

1. The clause of the Tallmadge proviso that forbade the further introduction of slavery into Missouri. It passed the House on February 17, 1819, by a vote of 87 to 76, and was rejected in the Senate on February 27 by a vote of 22 to 16.
2. The clause of the Tallmadge proviso that freed slave children born after the date of admission when they had reached the age of twenty-five. It passed the House on February 17, 1819, by a vote of 82 to 78, and was rejected in the Senate on February 27 by a vote of 31 to 7.
3. The Thomas amendment prohibiting slavery "forever" in that part of the Louisiana Purchase lying north of 36° 30′ (Missouri excepted). It was approved in the Senate on Febru-

ary 17, 1820, by a vote of 14 to 8, and passed the House on March 2 by a vote of 134 to 42.
4. The admission of California to statehood, which passed the Senate on August 13, 1850, by a vote of 34 to 18, and passed the House on September 7 by a vote of 150 to 56.
5. The organization of Utah Territory without any slavery restriction. It passed the Senate on July 31, 1850, by a vote of 32 to 18, and passed the House on September 7 by a vote of 97 to 85.
6. The organization of New Mexico Territory without any slavery restriction. It passed the Senate on August 15, 1850, by a vote of 27 to 10, and passed the House (where it was linked with the Senate bill settling the problems of the Texas debt and boundary) on September 6 by a vote of 108 to 97.
7. Abolition of the slave trade in the District of Columbia, passed by the Senate on September 16, 1850, by a vote of 33 to 19, and passed by the House on September 17, by a vote of 124 to 59.
8. The Fugitive Slave Act, passed by the Senate on August 23, 1850, by a vote of 27 to 12, and passed by the House on September 12 by a vote of 109 to 76.

Southern Congressional Voting on Slavery in 1819–1820 and 1850
(House and Senate Combined)

	Lower South	Middle South	Border South	Totals
Tallmadge–1	0–18	0–43	1–22	1–83
Tallmadge–2	0–18	0–43	2–20	2–81
36° 30′	12–14	17–29	22–2	51–45
California	1–39	11–29	21–6	33–74
Utah	23–12	31–4	23–1	77–17
New Mexico	15–19	29–10	24–1	68–30
D.C.	1–33	3–33	6–12	10–78
Fug. Slave	38–0	41–0	23–0	102–0

Notes

Introduction

1. David Donald, "American Historians and the Causes of the Civil War," *South Atlantic Quarterly*, LIX (1960), 351.
2. Avery O. Craven, *An Historian and the Civil War* (Chicago: University of Chicago Press, 1964), 1.
3. Joel H. Silbey, "The Civil War Synthesis in American Political History," *Civil War History*, X (1964), 140.
4. Eric Foner, "The Causes of the American Civil War: Recent Interpretations and New Directions," *Civil War History*, XX (1974), 197–98, 201–203.
5. Craven, *An Historian and the Civil War*, 232–33.
6. Foner, "Causes of the Civil War," 203.
7. Carl N. Degler, "The Two Cultures and the Civil War," in Stanley Coben and Lorman Ratner (eds.), *The Development of an American Culture* (Englewood Cliffs, N.J.: Prentice Hall, 1970), 92.
8. David Brion Davis, *The Problem of Slavery in Western Culture* (Ithaca, N.Y.: Cornell University Press, 1966); and *The Problem of Slavery in the Age of Revolution, 1770–1823* (Ithaca, N.Y.: Cornell University Press, 1975).
9. William L. Barney, *The Secessionist Impulse: Alabama and Mississippi in 1860* (Princeton: Princeton University Press, 1974), 313.
10. South Carolina, because of its experience with nullification, its premier leadership in secession, and its central role in the Fort Sumter crisis, might very well be treated as a category all by itself. In South Carolina, slaves were 57 percent of the population in 1860.

11. Avery O. Craven, *The Growth of Southern Nationalism, 1848–1861* (Baton Rouge: Louisiana State University Press, 1953), x.

12. The Georgia platform, a series of resolutions adopted by a convention called to consider the Compromise of 1850, named the following potential actions of Congress as sufficient in each case to justify secession: (1) abolition of slavery in the District of Columbia without the consent of its inhabitants; (2) abolition on federally owned property in the South; (3) suppression of the domestic slave trade; (4) refusal to admit a new slave state; (5) prohibition of slavery in the territories of New Mexico and Utah; (6) repeal or significant modification of the fugitive-slave laws.

Chapter 1

1. James A. Woodburn, "The Historical Significance of the Missouri Compromise," in *Annual Report of the American Historical Association for 1893* (Washington, D.C.: American Historical Association, 1894), 294.

2. Clement Eaton, *A History of the Old South* (2nd ed.; New York: Macmillan, 1966), 4.

3. Charles S. Sydnor, *The Development of Southern Sectionalism, 1819–1848* (Baton Rouge: Louisiana State University Press, 1948), 32.

4. Jesse T. Carpenter, *The South as a Conscious Minority, 1789–1861* (New York: New York University Press, 1930), 4.

5. John Richard Alden, *The First South* (Baton Rouge: Louisiana State University Press, 1961), 4.

6. Jefferson to John Taylor, June 1, 1798, in Paul Leicester Ford (ed.), *The Writings of Thomas Jefferson* (10 vols; New York: G. P. Putnam's Sons, 1892–99), VII, 263.

7. Jefferson to Stephens Thompson Mason, October 11, 1798, in *ibid.*, VII, 283.

8. *Annals of Congress*, 8th Cong., 2nd Sess., 1567–70.

9. For the rationalization of his silence on slavery during the presidential years, see Jefferson to George Logan, May 11, 1805, Ford (ed.), *Writings of Jefferson*, VIII, 351–52. On the subject generally, see John Chester Miller, *The Wolf by the Ears: Thomas Jefferson and Slavery* (New York: Free Press, 1977).

10. *Annals of Congress*, 8th Cong., 1st Sess., 241–42; Don E. Fehrenbacher, *The Dred Scott Case: Its Significance in American Law and Politics* (New York: Oxford University Press, 1978), 91–100.

11. *Annals of Congress*, 15th Cong., 1st Sess., 1675–76.

12. In New York especially, Republican factionalism strengthened the influence of dying Federalism. The followers of Governor DeWitt Clinton, widely regarded as Federalists at heart, lent strong support to the antislavery movement. See Shaw Livermore, Jr., *The Twilight of Federalism: The Disin-*

tegration of the Federalist Party, 1815–1830 (Princeton: Princeton University Press, 1962), 69–74; Glover Moore, *The Missouri Controversy, 1819–1821* (Lexington: University of Kentucky Press, 1966), 16–17.

13. Thomas D. Morris, *Free Men All: The Personal Liberty Laws of the North, 1780–1861* (Baltimore: Johns Hopkins University Press, 1974), 35–41; *Annals of Congress*, 15th Cong., 2nd Sess., 306, 311.

14. Southerners voted sixty-six to one against the first clause of the Tallmadge proviso and sixty-four to two against the second. Moore, *Missouri Controversy*, 53n.

15. *Annals of Congress*, 16th Cong., 1st Sess., 427, for the text of the 36° 30′ restriction, which is often called the Thomas Amendment because it was introduced by Jesse B. Thomas, Virginia-born senator from Illinois.

16. Moore, *Missouri Controversy*, 129–69.

17. *Annals of Congress*, 16th Cong., 1st Sess., 1391.

18. Ibid., 16th Cong., 1st Sess., 468, 1586–87.

19. Ibid., 16th Cong., 1st Sess., 428, 1587–88.

20. Moore, *Missouri Controversy*, 108.

21. Imprecise because it seems likely that some southern members of the House who voted against the 36° 30′ restriction by itself would have voted in favor of the Compromise package if they had had the opportunity. This, at least, was the case in the Senate, where southerners voted only fourteen to eight in favor of the 36° 30′ restriction, but twenty to two in favor of the Compromise as a whole. *Annals of Congress*, 16th Cong., 1st Sess., 428.

22. Moore, *Missouri Controversy*, 242.

23. Richmond *Enquirer*, February 10, 1820.

24. Moore, *Missouri Controversy*, 177.

25. *Annals of Congress*, 16th Cong., 1st Sess., 1578, 1582.

26. Ibid., 16th Cong., 1st Sess., 175; ibid., 15th Cong., 2nd Sess., 1204.

27. Richmond *Enquirer*, March 7, 1820.

28. Moore, *Missouri Controversy*, 175.

29. *Congressional Globe*, 35th Cong., 1st Sess., 773.

30. Moore, *Missouri Controversy*, 348.

31. *Annals of Congress*, 16th Cong., 1st Sess., 1025.

Chapter 2

1. *Congressional Globe*, 31st Cong., 1st Sess., 28, 1216.

2. Ibid., 31st Cong., 1st Sess., 259; Joseph Carlyle Sitterson, *The Secession Movement in North Carolina* (Chapel Hill: University of North Carolina Press, 1939), 69–70; Ulrich B. Phillips (ed.), *The Correspondence of Robert Toombs, Alexander H. Stephens, and Howell Cobb*, in *Annual Report of the American Historical Association for 1911* (2 vols.; Washington, D.C.: Ameri-

can Historical Association, 1912), II, 183; Jefferson Davis, *The Rise and Fall of the Confederate Government* (2 vols.; New York: D. Appleton, 1881), I, 83.
 3. *Congressional Globe*, 29th Cong., 2nd Sess., 454.
 4. Missouri was admitted August 10, 1821; the Wilmot Proviso was introduced August 8, 1846.
 5. Beveridge to Beard, March 16, 1926, Albert J. Beveridge Papers, Manuscript Division, Library of Congress.
 6. Chauncey C. Boucher and Robert P. Brooks (eds.), *Correspondence Addressed to John C. Calhoun, 1837–1849*, in *Annual Report of the American Historical Association for 1929* (2 vols.; Washington, D.C.: American Historical Association, 1930), II, 385–87.
 7. *Congressional Globe*, 31st Cong., 1st Sess., 235.
 8. *Ibid.*, 36th Cong., 2nd Sess., 56.
 9. *Ibid.*, 31st Cong., 1st Sess., 236.
 10. Henry Steele Commager (ed.), *Documents of American History* (7th ed.; 2 vols.; New York: Appleton-Century-Crofts, 1963), I, 373–74.
 11. Richmond *Enquirer*, February 19, 1847.
 12. *Congressional Globe*, 31st Cong., 1st Sess., 29. See also William J. Cooper, Jr., *The South and the Politics of Slavery, 1828–1856* (Baton Rouge: Louisiana State University Press, 1978), 240.
 13. Arthur Bestor, "State Sovereignty and Slavery: A Reinterpretation of Proslavery Constitutional Doctrine, 1846–1860," *Journal of the Illinois State Historical Society*, LIV (1961), 147.
 14. *Congressional Globe*, 29th Cong., 2nd Sess., 455, for Calhoun's resolutions of February 19, 1847.
 15. *Ibid.*, 29th Cong., 2nd Sess., 187; *ibid.*, 30th Cong., 1st Sess., 1062–63; Don E. Fehrenbacher, *The Dred Scott Case: Its Significance in American Law and Politics* (New York: Oxford University Press, 1978), 132–33, 147–51.
 16. David M. Potter, *The Impending Crisis, 1848–1861*, completed and edited by Don E. Fehrenbacher (New York: Harper and Row, 1976), 73–75; Robert W. Johannsen, *Stephen A. Douglas* (New York: Oxford University Press, 1973), 242.
 17. *Congressional Globe*, 31st Cong., 1st Sess., 203.
 18. Richard Malcolm Johnston and William Hand Browne (eds.), *Life of Alexander H. Stephens* (rev. ed.; Philadelphia: J. B. Lippincott, 1883), 238–39.
 19. Holman Hamilton, *Prologue to Conflict: The Crisis and Compromise of 1850* (Lexington: University of Kentucky Press, 1964), 54.
 20. Fehrenbacher, *Dred Scott Case*, 162–63. Tables of voting are in Hamilton, *Prologue to Conflict*, 191–200.
 21. Phillips (ed.), *Correspondence of Toombs, Stephens, and Cobb*, 283.
 22. Robert R. Russel, "What Was the Compromise of 1850?" *Journal of*

Southern History, XXII (1956), 292–309. For a critique, see Fehrenbacher, *Dred Scott Case*, 174–76.

23. *Harper's New Monthly Magazine*, IV (1851), 120, calculated that recent elections in the four states had resulted in 110,882 secessionist votes out of a total of 261,388 (about 42 percent). But see Cooper, *South and the Politics of Slavery*, 309, where it is maintained that the elections were not a confrontation between Unionists and disunionists.

24. Phillips (ed.), *Correspondence of Toombs, Stephens, and Cobb*, 249–59.

25. Potter, *Impending Crisis*, 143–44.

26. Richard Harrison Shryock, *Georgia and the Union in 1850* (Durham, N.C.: Duke University Press, 1926), 344.

Chapter 3

1. *Congressional Globe*, 27th Cong., 3rd Sess., App., 103.

2. Jesse T. Carpenter, *The South as a Conscious Minority, 1789–1861* (New York: New York University Press, 1930), 180–81.

3. David M. Potter, *The Impending Crisis, 1848–1861*, completed and edited by Don E. Fehrenbacher (New York: Harper and Row, 1976), 235–38, but cf. Michael F. Holt, *The Political Crisis of the 1850's* (New York: John Wiley and Sons, 1978), 102, 118–19. Holt advances a striking new thesis that the second American party system collapsed in the 1850s "because Whig and Democratic voters lost faith in their old parties as adequate vehicles for effective political action."

4. See Potter, *Impending Crisis*, 238–47; Holt, *Political Crisis*, 154–69.

5. John V. Mering, "The Slave-State Constitutional Unionists and the Politics of Consensus," *Journal of Southern History*, XLIII (1977), 398. See also William J. Cooper, Jr., *The South and the Politics of Slavery, 1828–1856* (Baton Rouge: Louisiana State University Press, 1978), 372–73.

6. *Congressional Globe*, 33rd Cong., 1st Sess., 1254; Potter, *Impending Crisis*, 167n.

7. William L. Barney, *The Road to Secession: A New Perspective on the Old South* (New York: Praeger Publishers, 1972), 6, and William L. Barney, *The Secessionist Impulse: Alabama and Mississippi in 1860* (Princeton: Princeton University Press, 1974), 16.

8. Don E. Fehrenbacher, "Disunion and Reunion," in John Higham (ed.), *The Reconstruction of American History* (New York: Harper and Row, 1962), 102.

9. Avery O. Craven, *The Growth of Southern Nationalism, 1848–1861* (Baton Rouge: Louisiana State University Press, 1953), 196. But cf. Cooper, *The South and the Politics of Slavery*, 352n, where Craven's interpretation is disputed.

10. Craven, *Growth of Southern Nationalism*, 394.
11. George Harmon Knoles (ed.), *The Crisis of the Union, 1860–1861* (Baton Rouge: Louisiana State University Press, 1965), 88.
12. The support of the Lower South was in fact unanimous. Of the 145 anti-Lecompton votes in both houses, 10 were cast by southerners—8 from the Border South and 2 from the Middle South. *Congressional Globe*, 35th Cong., 1st Sess., 1264–65, 1437.
13. *Ibid.*, 35th Cong., 1st Sess., 393.
14. *Ibid.*, 35th Cong., 1st Sess., 858.
15. James D. Tradewell to Hammond, February 11, 1858, James H. Hammond Papers, Manuscript Division, Library of Congress.
16. James D. Richardson (ed.), *A Compilation of the Messages and Papers of the Presidents* (11 vols.; Washington: Government Printing Office, 1913), IV, 3011.
17. W. D. Porter to James H. Hammond, January 30, 1858, Hammond Papers.
18. Ulrich B. Phillips (ed.), *The Correspondence of Robert Toombs, Alexander H. Stephens, and Howell Cobb*, in *Annual Report of the American Historical Association for 1911* (2 vols.; Washington, D.C.: American Historical Association, 1912), II, 432, 434.
19. Richardson (ed.), *Messages and Papers of the Presidents*, IV, 2963.
20. See above, p. 7.
21. Joseph Carlyle Sitterson, *The Secession Movement in North Carolina* (Chapel Hill: University of North Carolina Press, 1939), 135.
22. John Bassett Moore (ed.), *The Works of James Buchanan* (12 vols.; Philadelphia: Lippincott, 1908–11), X, 229.
23. Robert W. Johannsen, *Stephen A. Douglas* (New York: Oxford University Press, 1973), 685–87.
24. Don E. Fehrenbacher, *The Dred Scott Case: Its Influence in American Law and Politics* (New York: Oxford University Press, 1978), 468, 483–84.
25. W. D. Porter to James H. Hammond, December 28, 1857, Hammond Papers; Charleston *Mercury*, January 16, 1858. For other similar comments, see Harold S. Schultz, *Nationalism and Sectionalism in South Carolina, 1852–1860* (Durham, N.C.: Duke University Press, 1950), 168–69.
26. Ollinger Crenshaw, *The Slave States in the Presidential Election of 1860* (Baltimore: Johns Hopkins Press, 1945), 104*n*.
27. July 10, 1860, in Dwight Lowell Dumond (ed.), *Southern Editorials on Secession* (New York: Century, 1931), 141.
28. Charleston *Mercury*, April 20, 21, 1857.
29. Potter, *Impending Crisis*, 325–26.

Constitutions and Constitutionalism in the Slaveholding South

Preface

"If we investigate the origins of modern Constitutions," wrote the British scholar Kenneth Weare some years ago, "we find that, practically without exception, they were drawn up and adopted because people wished to make a fresh start." The desire for a fresh start, as Weare noted, has often been associated with revolution. England, for instance, experimented briefly with written constitutions during the 1650s, after seven years of civil war had culminated in the execution of Charles I. Similarly, the two constitutions of the United States were adopted in the 1780s, during and soon after a successful rebellion against British authority. Another American constitution, drafted in 1861 by delegates gathered at Montgomery, Alabama, was likewise infused with revolutionary purpose, signaling as it did the determination of one part of the nation to separate itself from the rest.

Thus, at the national level of government, American constitutional history appears to bear out Weare's generalization. At the state level, however, one finds a different pattern. There, constitution-making, although it too began as a revolutionary enterprise, came to be part of the ordinary political process. The difference is especially significant with respect to the South; for in national constitutional history the southern role has usually been perceived as one of aberrance, whereas in state constitutional development the South has been well within the American mainstream. Accordingly, when I was invited to give the Lamar Memorial Lectures at Mercer University on a subject appropriate for the bicentennial year, I decided, perhaps overambitiously, to include both state and national levels of government in a survey of southern constitutionalism during the slaveholding era. The results of the undertaking are imprinted on the pages that follow. In their preparation, I have as usual had much help from my wife, Virginia, who joins me in thanking Wayne and Frances Mixon, Henry and Patricia Warnock, and those other members of the university community who extended us such a warm welcome to the Mercer campus and to the historic city of Macon.

Don E. Fehrenbacher

One

Southern State Constitutions

American independence had been confirmed by treaty for less than five years when the Constitutional Convention began its work at Philadelphia in May of 1787. Yet the foundations of American constitutionalism were already well laid, resting as they did on a rich heritage of European political thought, on the English legal tradition, and on American colonial and Revolutionary experience. By "constitutionalism," I mean a complex of ideas, attitudes, and patterns of behavior elaborating the principle that the authority of government derives from and is limited by a body of fundamental law. For Americans, distinctively, the word "constitution" had come to mean a single document embodying the sovereign will of the people—a document that established or reorganized a government, prescribing its structure and endowing it with power, while at the same time restricting that power in the interest of personal liberty.

The earliest constitution-making in America was undertaken, not for the new nation, but for the constituent parts of the new nation as they individually suspended or renounced their allegiance to Great Britain. It was an enterprise to which many Revolutionary leaders enthusiastically turned their hands. "Nothing," writes Gordon Wood, "—not the creation of this confederacy, not the Continental Congress, not the war, not the French alliance—in the years surrounding the Declaration of Independence engaged the interests of Americans more than the framing of these separate governments."[1] Procedures varied a good deal from state to state in those first efforts, but by 1787 it was becoming accepted doctrine that a constitution ought to be framed by a convention elected solely for that purpose.[2] By 1787 it had also been demonstrated in several state court decisions that a constitution as fundamental law was not merely hortatory but could be enforced by judicial invalidation of legislative action.[3]

Thus it was at the state level of government that Americans introduced written constitutions to the world, at the state level that they invented the constitutional convention and first experimented with judicial review. In addition, it was at the state level that a bill of rights came to be regarded as a necessary part of any constitution, and at the state level that American political leaders first tried to actualize the principle of separation of powers. State constitutional development in the formative years has always received some measure of scholarly attention, but its great historical importance is largely obscured by the splendor of the achievement at Philadelphia in 1787. Out of a hundred persons who can identify James Madison as the putative "Father of the Constitution," could more than half a dozen name the principal author of the oldest written constitution still in operation?[4] And how many would know anything at all about later state constitutional history? That is completely *terra incognita* for most Americans, in spite of the fact that until well after the Civil War, state governments had considerably more influence than the Federal government on social institutions, economic enterprise, and the quality of American life.

There is no satisfactory general history of state constitutional development from the Revolution to the Civil War. In fact, multi-state treatments of any kind are exceedingly rare. Among them, Fletcher M. Green's study of five South Atlantic states, published some sixty years ago, still stands by itself.[5] To extend one's range in a single essay over more ground than Green ventured to cover in his entire book is perhaps a dubious undertaking. Nevertheless, even so brief a review of constitution-making and constitutional change in the fifteen slaveholding states may serve as a useful introduction to this neglected subject. In addition, it may contribute something relevant to the everlasting debate over southern distinctiveness.

Let us examine three aspects of southern state constitutional development from 1776 to 1861: 1) the relation between the government and the people as manifested in the process of constitution-making and in arrangements for suffrage and representation; 2) the constitutional structure of government, with particular emphasis on the allocation and limitation of governmental power; and 3) the substantive content introduced into some state constitutions by way of determining certain public policies and placing them beyond the reach of ordinary legislation.

The first American constitutions were written in 1776 and 1777 to regularize the provisional governments that had already emerged in every colony as a result of the Revolutionary crisis. Congress encouraged such action but did not respond to the suggestion that it draft a standard constitution for all states.[6] For the various groups of framers from New Hampshire to Georgia, procedural guidelines were almost wholly lacking, and there was little help in the way of models other than the colonial charters. Circumstances had made these men constitutional pioneers, but what the critical times demanded was the speedy establishment of a workable system of government in each state, without elaborate concern about constitutional theory. It is not at all clear, for instance, that the authors of the first state constitutions generally understood themselves to be writing fundamental law of a kind that would impose legally enforceable limitations on legislative power. Such understanding came with accumulating experience in self-government and with reflection upon that experience.[7]

The constitutions of South Carolina and Virginia were drafted and adopted by their Revolutionary assemblies in the manner of ordinary legislation, without express authorization from the people. The constitutions of Delaware, Maryland, North Carolina, and Georgia were drafted by conventions elected for that purpose, but each of these bodies also acted in some degree as a legislature, thus blurring the distinction between constitution and statute. In Delaware, however, the convention's legislative activity was so limited that it could perhaps be regarded as the first true constitutional convention.[8]

Three of the first southern constitutions lasted well into the nineteenth century, but South Carolina adopted a second one in 1778 and a third in 1790; Georgia, a second in 1789 and a third in 1798; and Delaware a second in 1792. In addition, Kentucky and Tennessee were admitted to the Union in the 1790s, having drafted acceptable constitutions, and Kentucky acquired its second fundamental instrument in 1799. The South Carolina legislature framed the state's constitution of 1778, but thereafter, every southern constitution was the work of a convention elected for that purpose alone. On the other hand, despite the examples set by Massachusetts in 1780 and New Hampshire in 1784, none of the fourteen southern constitutions adopted before 1800 were submitted to the electorate for ratification. Georgia came the closest to such action in 1788–89, when three separately elected conventions drafted a constitution, proposed amendments to it, and ratified the amended document.[9] Not until 1821 did a state outside of New England (namely, New York) hold a referendum on a proposed constitution. Nine years later, Virginia became the first southern state to do so, and from then until 1860, submission was the prevailing practice in the South.[10] Of course the practice entailed the risk that the work of a convention might go for naught. Thus, Missouri voters rejected a new constitution in 1846, and Delaware voters did the same in 1853.[11]

During the period 1800 to 1860, seven more slaveholding states entered the Union, each with a constitution acceptable to Congress, and nine new constitutions were adopted by seven southern states already in the Union.[12] Of those sixteen constitutions, Louisiana was responsible for three, Virginia and Mississippi for two apiece, and nine other states for one apiece. North Carolina, South Carolina, and Georgia continued to get along with their eighteenth-century frames of government, although each underwent some change by amendment. During the same sixty-year period, by way of comparison, ten free states entered the Union, each with an acceptable constitution, and a total of twelve new constitutions were adopted by ten free states already in the Union. Of those twenty-two documents, seven states were responsible for two apiece and eight for one apiece.[13] Three New England states continued to get along with their eighteenth-century constitutions. Plainly, there were more similarities than differences in the sectional patterns of constitution-making.

By 1860, North Carolina was the only state in the Union with a constitution dating back to 1776. Even that document had been substantially revised in 1835, despite the fact that nothing in its text gave authority for such revision. A convention was called by the legislature on its own authority, and that convention drafted a number of amendments, which were then approved in a referendum. One of the additions was a provision for future amendment of the constitution by a process involving the approval of two successive legislatures and submission to popular ratification.[14] Revision of this kind, by amendment originating in legislative action, had been provided for as early as 1776 in the first constitutions of Maryland and Delaware. On the other hand, the first Georgia constitution authorized its own revision by a convention called in response to petitions signed by a majority of voters in a majority of the state's counties.[15] All southern state constitutions written from 1777 to 1860, except those of Virginia, contained provisions for amendment by extraordinary legislative action or by convention or sometimes by either means.[16] Many important constitutional changes were made by amendment. It is therefore misleading, for example, to say that Georgians in 1860 still lived under a constitution adopted in 1798; for amendments had been added to the document in 1808, 1812, 1818, 1819, 1824, 1833, 1835, 1840, 1841, 1843, 1847, and 1849—amendments dealing with such subjects as legislative apportionment, frequency of elections, qualifications for office, and gubernatorial succession. There was also an amendment eliminating legislative divorce and another that belatedly created a state supreme court, which Georgia did without until 1845.[17]

Of course, state constitutions also underwent much change of meaning, without alteration of text, as a result of legislative and judicial construction. But it is in the amount of formal change that American constitutional history differs so strikingly at the state and national levels. After ratification of the Twelfth Amendment in 1804, the Federal Constitution remained untouched for sixty-one years. During that period, only two amendments were passed by Congress and submitted for ratification—one in 1810 and the other in 1861.[18] The states, in comparison, were veritable beehives of constitutional activity, exemplifying the Jeffersonian principle that every generation should write its own fundamental law.[19] Even South Carolina, in many respects the most conservative of states, added a number of significant amendments to its constitution during the two decades preceding the Nullification controversy. In 1810, for instance, the property qualification for voting was virtually replaced with a six-month residence requirement.[20]

Furthermore, the framing and revision of southern state constitutions came to involve popular participation at several stages of the enterprise. Beginning with provisions in the Delaware, Kentucky, and Tennessee constitutions of the 1790s, it became a common practice for legislatures to submit the question of calling a constitutional convention to a vote of the people.[21] If they approved of the call, there followed an election of delegates to the convention. When its work was done, antebellum voters more often than not went to the polls for a third time to pass judgment on the new constitution or on proposed amendments to the old one. In these procedures of constitution-making, Americans were acting out the principle of popular sovereignty, which locates the source of all governmental power in the will of the people. Those Americans responsible for the drafting of state constitutions had to wrestle with the correlative principle of popular consent, which requires that the exercise of governmental power be subject to the periodic approval of the people. Between the Revolution and the Civil War, there was extensive progress toward the democratization of political consent in the United States—most of it achieved through state constitutional change.

"Consent of the people," as an operative political principle, means consent of the electorate, whose membership, undefined by the United States Constitution, was left for the individual states to specify. At the beginning of the Revolution, all of the thirteen original states had property-owning or taxpaying qualifications for voting. In many states there were also special property and religious qualifications for holding office.[22] These restrictions, reflecting eighteenth-century views of the appropriate political constituency and the sources of public virtue, began to disappear even before 1800, but some of them were still in effect at the outbreak of the Civil War.

Of the fifteen slaveholding states, only South Carolina's constitution ever contained a religious qualification for voting, and that lasted only from 1778 to 1790.[23] But for varying lengths of time, eight southern states had religious qualifications for officeholding. Some of them required an adherence to Protestantism; others, an adherence to Christianity; and still others, just belief in God and a future state of rewards and punishments.[24] Soon after ratification of the Federal Constitution, which prohibited religious tests for national office, the qualifications were removed from the constitutions of Georgia, South Carolina, and Delaware.[25] Some slackening of restrictions was also eventually achieved in Maryland and North Carolina, but those two states, along with Tennessee, Mississippi, and Arkansas, retained some kind of religious qualification for officeholding throughout the antebellum period.[26] It appears, however, that the tests were, for the most part, more aggravating as social symbols than effective as political barriers. In the North Carolina convention of 1835, for instance, there was a heavy attack on the article excluding from office any person who denied the truth of the Protestant religion. The leader of the onslaught, who succeeded in getting the word "Protestant" changed to "Christian," was William Gaston, a Catholic recently elected to the state supreme court after having served eleven terms in the legislature. During the convention debates it was generally acknowledged that the restrictive article had probably never kept any person out of office in North Carolina.[27]

The elitist view of political leadership prevailing at the time of the Revolution was given emphatic expression in property qualifications for holding office that exceeded—and often far exceeded—the qualifications for suffrage. Eight of the first ten southern states had such restrictions in their early constitutions.[28] For example, a man could vote in Maryland if he owned a fifty-acre freehold or other property worth £30, but he needed a £500 estate to serve in the House of Delegates; a £1,000 estate to serve in the Senate; and a £5,000 estate to become governor. Virginia was unique among southern states in having identical freehold requirements for suffrage and officeholding, both of which continued in force until 1851.[29] Kentucky was for many years unique among southern states in having no property qualifications at all. But overt elitism began to go out of fashion in the Jeffersonian era, and only one southern constitution written after 1817 contained a special property test for holding office. That was the Delaware constitution of 1831, which omitted the old freehold requirement for admission to the lower house, but retained the provision that a member of the Senate must own 200 acres or other property worth £1000.[30] By the time of the Civil War, Delaware, North Carolina, and South Carolina were the only southern states still clinging to restrictions of this kind.[31]

Much more controversial and significant than the decline of special qualifications for officeholding were various constitutional changes broadening the franchise. For many states, an intermediate stage of liberalization was the establishment of a taxpaying requirement in place of, or as an alternative to, a propertyholding requirement. Of the six original southern states, Georgia and South Carolina had passed through the taxpaying stage to universal white male suffrage by 1810. Delaware adopted a taxpaying requirement in 1792 and retained it throughout the antebellum period. Maryland abolished its property qualification outright in 1810, but another forty years passed before Virginia did the same. North Carolina's 1776 constitution established taxpaying as the basic qualification for suffrage, but with a propertyholding requirement for electors of the state senate. This curious dual system was not abolished until 1856.[32] Of the non-original southern states, none ever adopted a propertyholding qualification.[33] Louisiana and Mississippi had taxpaying qualifications for a while, but the other seven embraced universal suffrage from the beginning.[34]

It seems likely that at any time after 1810, more southerners were being disfranchised by the standard residence requirements of up to two years than by the remaining property and taxpaying qualifications. One should bear in mind, moreover, that the effectiveness of constitutional restrictions on the franchise varied according to the strictness of local enforcement. Without voter registration laws, such enforcement was especially difficult in places of rapid population change, and everywhere it came to depend largely upon party vigilance at the polls. As for sectional differences in the progress of suffrage reform, they do not appear to have been very significant. In 1840, for instance, two southern states and one northern state still had property qualifications, while two other southern and six other northern states had taxpaying qualifications, some of which were little more than nominal.[35]

The democratic implications in an expanding suffrage were also manifested in a trend toward more elective offices. Governors, judges, and local officials, commonly chosen by the legislature at the beginning of the nineteenth century, were in most states elected by the people on the eve of the

Civil War. There was more than a spirit of democracy at work in these changes, however, for popular election also served the eighteenth-century republican purpose of chastening and diffusing power in the hope of securing better government. Of course the great exception to the general trend was aristocratic South Carolina. There, suffrage meant little more than the privilege of electing the members of an omnipotent legislature, which in 1860 still chose nearly all state and local officials, including even the presidential electors.[36] Thus the right to vote was one thing; how much that vote counted was another matter.

While suffrage requirements designated the constituent members of the political order, it was the structure of representation that allocated power within that membership. In a number of southern states—especially Virginia and the Carolinas, where the western regions were notoriously underrepresented—the issue of legislative apportionment was as controversial as the issue of suffrage during the first half of the nineteenth century.[37] The various struggles involved not only intrastate sectional rivalries but partisan, class, and urban-rural conflicts as well, and they also posed the familiar question of how slavery fitted into a design of republican government.

Both the Massachusetts constitution of 1780 and the New Hampshire constitution of 1784 apportioned representation in the state senate according to taxes paid. The constitution adopted in 1790 by Pennsylvania apportioned representation in both houses of the legislature according to taxable inhabitants. Except, however, for a provision in the South Carolina constitution of 1778 that never went into effect,[38] none of the early southern state constitutions contained general formulas of apportionment. Instead, they specifically assigned legislative seats to counties, towns, parishes, and other districts, usually on a basis of equality in the upper house but with population, or population and property, taken loosely into account for the lower house. Thus, the North Carolina constitution allotted each county one senator and two representatives, but awarded an additional representative to each of six towns; and the Georgia constitution of 1789 allotted each county one senator and from two to five representatives.[39]

Apportionment of this kind, prescribed specifically in the constitution itself without provision for adjustment to demographic change, was bound to be a source of much discontent in the four states that clung to it for more than half a century—namely, Delaware, Maryland, Virginia, and North Carolina. From 1792 onward, however, most new southern constitutions contained general rules for apportionment and periodic reapportionment by legislative action, with population as the basis in one house or both.[40] But in framing such rules, constitution-makers were forced to consider certain theoretical aspects of representation and make some fundamental choices. Of central importance in the South was the question whether legislative apportionment should be based upon the whole population, as many slaveholders desired, or upon the free population, as non-slaveholders generally preferred. That problem, resolved at the national level in 1787 by the famous three-fifths compromise, remained a provocative issue in southern constitutional politics throughout the antebellum period.

The clear preference was for representation based on the free population or some comparable category that excluded slaves, such as white population, free male population, white male population, or qualified voters.[41] That, of course, was what northerners had supported and southerners had opposed in the Federal Convention. No state opted for apportionment according to the whole population, including slaves, until Louisiana and Maryland elected to do so in the 1840s and 1850s.[42] Only Georgia and Florida, together with Maryland for a few years and North Carolina after 1834, made use of the three-fifths formula, or "federal number," as it was sometimes called.[43]

The fiercest battle over suffrage and representation took place in the most famous of all state constitutional conventions—the one that assembled at Richmond in October 1829, with a distinguished roll of delegates that included two former Presidents, one future President, and the incumbent Chief Justice of the United States. For more than three months, the state capitol that Jefferson had designed was the scene of a great running debate on the nature of man, the theory and practice of government, and the consideration owed to property. The conservative argument presented by Tidewater and Piedmont planters was freighted with political realism. "The safety of men depends upon the safety of property," declared Abel P. Upshur, a member of the state supreme court and later secretary of state. "It must be manifest by this time . . . that property is entitled to protection, and that *our* property [meaning slaves in particular] imperiously demands *that kind of protection* which flows from the possession of power."[44] The reform elements in the convention, largely from the western part of the state, had the advantage of appealing to political idealism and of being able to cite constitutional trends elsewhere. "Virginia and North Carolina," said one man, "are the only States that adhere to the freehold test, and the latter only in one branch of the Legislature. . . . is Virginia less fit for free Government than her sister States?"[45]

In the end, the Virginia reformers of 1829–30 secured only modification rather than abolition of the property qualification, and they were just marginally successful in their struggle for a more equitable apportionment.[46] Twenty-one years later, another constitutional convention readily installed universal white male suffrage, but the problem of representation still defied resolution, and the delegates had to settle for makeshift. The constitution of 1851 arbitrarily apportioned legislative seats in such a way as to give eastern Virginia control of the Senate and western Virginia control of the House. Determination of a permanent principle of representation was postponed for fourteen years and left to legislative discretion or, as a last resort, to the will of the people expressed in a referendum.[47]

The persistent constitutional conservatism of Virginia and North Carolina was sustained by many influences, not the least among them being the weight of political inertia and the pull of historical tradition. Perhaps the most important factor, however, was an acute sense of insecurity that made the intrenched planter class unwilling to accept "Herrenvolk democracy." In both states and in Tennessee as well, the plantation elite feared majority rule because the nonslaveholding majority of the population included an element, both numerous and geographically concentrated, that was hostile to slavery. The principal danger apprehended was not abolitionism but "oppressive" taxation directed at slave property. A Piedmont delegate to the Virginia convention summed up the conservative view with this pronouncement: "No Government can be just, or wise, or safe for Virginia, which shall place the property of the East in the power and at the disposal of the West."[48] As for North Carolina, taxation of slaves was a divisive issue in the constitutional convention of 1835, and it became more bitterly so on the eve of the Civil War, when reformers proposed to introduce the ad valorem principle.[49] "This movement," wrote one conservative, "contains the mischievous elements of Seward's 'irrepressible conflict,' brought home to us."[50]

Constitutional provisions for suffrage and representation allocated electoral power and thereby specified the connections between government and popular consent. At the same time, a much larger part of the constitutional text was usually devoted to the structure of state government and the allocation of power among its parts. Of the first southern constitutions, four expressly embraced the principle of separation of powers, and the other two implicitly paid it a measure of respect.[51] But in the struggles leading to the Revolution, the colonial assemblies had been the primary centers of American resistance to British authority, while the colonial governors had been the principal agents of the Crown and Parliament. Consequently, the practical effect universally achieved in the early constitutions was something close to legislative supremacy. In all six states, the governor or equivalent official was elected by the legislature for a term as short as one year. He had no significant appointive power except in Maryland and no veto power except briefly in South Carolina.[52] Moreover, he was subject in varying degrees to the restraint of an executive council. Governor Edmund Randolph of Virginia referred to himself in 1786 as merely "a member of the executive."[53] Aside from the periodic control exercised by the electorate, the principal restraint on legislative power was the internal one of bicameralism, adopted by five southern states in 1776, but not by Georgia until the writing of its second constitution in 1789.[54]

Widespread dissatisfaction with the state governments of the Revolutionary period inspired considerable reaction against legislative supremacy—a reaction articulated in the writings of Jefferson and Madison and plainly visible in the Constitution of the United States.[55] Most of the later state constitutions achieved a better balance between the three branches of government, but nowhere did the amount of executive power or the degree of judicial independence ever equal that introduced into the Federal system.

All nine southern states that entered the Union between 1792 and 1845 did so with constitutions that provided for popular election of the governor and all but Tennessee allowed him a qualified veto.[56] Most of the six original southern states were slow to follow suit. Until 1852, the Virginia legislature elected not only the governor but also a council of state, which the governor had to consult before exercising "any discretionary power conferred on him by the constitution and laws."[57] In 1860, the legislature of South Carolina was still choosing the state's governor and other executive officers, as well as its judges and presidential electors. At that same late date, five of the six governors still could not veto legislation, and only two had any significant control over appointments.[58] But then, a majority of the non-original states were likewise reluctant to lodge much appointive power with the governor. They preferred to have their state treasurers, state auditors, attorneys general, and other such officials elected either by the legislature or by the people. This decentralization of the executive branch of state government was, like bicameralism, an extension of the principle of separation of powers. It reflected the eighteenth-century view that authority could be rendered less dangerous by dividing it.

American constitutional theory in general and the doctrine of separation of powers in particular required the establishment of an independent judiciary. After all, judges made dependent on the King's will alone had been one of the great American complaints itemized by Jefferson in 1776. Nevertheless, judicial independence was only partly achieved in the early state constitutions, owing to the general tendency toward legislative domination. At the beginning of the Jacksonian era, eleven of the twelve southern states had supreme courts or the equivalent. Their members, chosen by the legislature or the governor, all held office during good behavior.[59] They were subject to impeachment and in many states could also be removed by "address" of two-thirds of the legislature for reasons other than those justifying impeachment, but efforts at removal by such means hardly ever succeeded.[60]

The fiercest legislative attacks upon the judiciary were directed not merely at punishing individual judges but at controlling the decisions of the supreme court or putting it out of business altogether. Thus, after the Kentucky court of appeals ruled against the constitutionality of a law for the relief of debtors, the legislature in 1824 "reorganized" the court by replacing it with a new one. The castoff judges responded defiantly by continuing to sit and hear appeals. After two years of constitutional turmoil, a new legislature repealed the reorganization act, thereby reinstating the old court and vindicating its independence.[61] Another case in point is the way the South Carolina legislature dealt with certain troublesome judges in the aftermath of the Nullification crisis. It simply abolished the state court of appeals as a separate body and restored an older system whereby the circuit judges assembled periodically to review their own decisions as a court of last resort. Not until 1859 was the court of appeals re-established.[62] These Kentucky and South Carolina episodes were exceptional, however, and for the most part, state supreme courts of the Jacksonian period were relatively secure from legislative coercion and reprisal.

In 1831, when Mississippi voters approved the calling of a constitutional convention, the idea of an elective judiciary had begun to make headway, and it proved to be the leading issue in the contest for delegate seats. After some warm debate on the convention floor, the "whole hogs" carried the day against the "aristocrats" like John A. Quitman, who argued in vain that the innovation would "strike a fatal blow at the independence of the judiciary."⁶³ Mississippi thus became the first state in the nation to experiment with popular election of its supreme court.⁶⁴ For almost two decades, the example was not followed anywhere in the South. Then, during the early 1850s, seven more southern states opted for an elected supreme court, which made the proportion in the South about the same as in the rest of the country.⁶⁵ By that time, moreover, lower court judges were popularly elected in eleven of the fifteen southern states.⁶⁶

As an influence on judicial independence, the difference between appointment and popular election was probably less important than the tenure of office. To Americans of the 1830s, election of anyone for life would have seemed absurdly contradictory, and so it is not surprising that the Mississippi constitution of 1832 should have accompanied popular election with a term of service set at six years.⁶⁷ Such limitation of tenure caught on more quickly than popular election. Indeed, Alabama had already adopted it by amendment, and Tennessee, Georgia, and Arkansas did so within four years. By 1860, twelve of the fifteen southern supreme courts had members serving terms ranging from six to twelve years.⁶⁸ Thus the democratic tendencies of the age seemed to have eroded judicial independence. Yet some advocates of popular election and limited terms for judges argued that the changes would strengthen the judiciary by rescuing it from dependence on the legislature and anchoring its authority in the periodic sanction of the people.⁶⁹

Perhaps the most distinctive feature of the American constitutional system is judicial review, the power of a court to invalidate legislation found to be in violation of fundamental law. State judges were bound by oath to enforce not only the constitution and laws of their respective states but also the Constitution, laws, and treaties of the United States.

Thus state court review was not confined to holding state legislation within the limits set by the state constitution. A state law could also be challenged in a state court on the grounds that it violated some part of the Federal Constitution, such as the contract clause or the privileges-and-immunities clause.

Never explicitly authorized in any antebellum constitution, the power of judicial review was asserted and exercised by a number of state courts even before John Marshall issued his classic statement on the subject in *Marbury v. Madison*.[70] A notable example is *Bayard v. Singleton*, decided by the high court of North Carolina in 1787. The fundamental question was whether the legislature had exceeded its authority when it passed a law requiring the dismissal of suits for recovery of confiscated Loyalist lands. The judges ruled that it had, and thus, for the first time in a reported American case, a court declared a statute to be void on the ground that it conflicted with the more fundamental law of a constitution.[71] The emergence of judicial review, although in some respects a logical consequence of American reliance on written constitutions, must also be viewed as part of the post-Revolutionary reaction against legislative supremacy. By 1815, courts in nearly all states, North and South, had invalidated statutes or at least asserted a right to do so.[72] In fact, it was already becoming commonplace for jurists to speak of the power and responsibility as too firmly established to be disputed. A Maryland judge rendering a decision in 1816 began with an elaborate essay demonstrating that judicial review could not be justified on any logical grounds. Then, acknowledging that the highest courts of Maryland and the United States had settled the question otherwise, he declared: "To this weight of authority, I feel myself therefore compelled to submit." After which, he proceeded to rule against the constitutionality of a Maryland statute.[73]

Although state courts often asserted the power of judicial review, they also commonly added that the power must always be used with restraint, and the instances in which they actually overturned significant legislation were not very numerous.[74] In the supreme court of Virginia, for example, the constitutionality of state legislation was tested more than twenty-five times before the Civil War, but only twice did the court actually invalidate a statute.[75] One of those two decisions involved the Virginia court system itself, and the other was not entirely free from judicial self-protectiveness.[76] In the South as a whole, constitutional cases arose less frequently than in Virginia but the proportion of invalidations was higher. A survey of approximately seventy-five such cases in twelve states reveals about thirty instances in which a law or part of a law was declared unconstitutional.[77] At least a third of those thirty decisions could be described as technical legal corrections, often of minor consequence. The others, spread over three-quarters of a century, dealt with a variety of matters that fell into no discernible overall pattern beyond a predominant concern with property rights. Among the subjects at issue were: fair compensation for land taken by eminent domain, repeal of a state land grant, forfeiture of land for nonpayment of taxes, legislative dismissal of certain classes of suits, stay-law relief for debtors, river navigation and the rights of mill owners, regulation of the possession of firearms, forfeiture of illegally imported slaves, the right of certain slaves to sue for freedom, and legislative procedure in amending the constitution.[78] As often as not, southern courts upheld legislation in the face of constitutional challenge, including, for example, a prohibitory liquor law, a workers' lien law, a lottery law, a law incorporating a state bank, a law authorizing a city to borrow money and lay taxes in support of internal improvements, and a law for construction and maintenance of levees along the Mississippi River.[79] On the whole, judicial review by southern state courts, though well established in theory and practice before 1860, was something less than a major curb on legislative power.

A collateral fact of some interest is that before the Civil War, although the opportunity more than once presented itself, no Virginia supreme court ever nullified legislation on the grounds that it violated the state's famous Declaration of Rights.[80] Elsewhere in the South, the record was marginally different. Most southern states followed Virginia's example in framing a declaration or bill of rights, which was usually placed at the beginning of the constitution. But the legal meaning of these noble pronouncements was at first not entirely clear. The ones written during the Revolution were couched in advisory language compatible with the prevalence of legislative supremacy. Thus the Maryland declaration stated that "no *ex post facto* law ought to be made," and that "excessive bail ought not to be required." One clause of the Virginia document asserted that free government could be preserved only "by a firm adherence to justice, moderation, temperance, frugality and virtue, and by frequent recurrence to fundamental principles."[81] Such words, said Alexander Hamilton, "would sound much better in a treatise of ethics than in a constitution of government."[82] By the 1790s, to be sure, the word "ought" was being replaced by "shall," and thereafter state bills of rights were usually phrased, like their Federal counterpart, in the language of legal command. Judicial enforcement was at first most vigorous in North Carolina and Kentucky, where, by 1805, laws had been declared unconstitutional on each of the following grounds: denying trial by jury, operating retrospectively, impairing the obligation of a contract, taking private property for public use without just compensation, and inflicting deprivation of property without due process of law.[83] In later years, the judicial rationale for judicial review tended increasingly to stress protection of individuals and minorities against the power of the majority.[84] It appears that over half the state laws invalidated by state courts before the Civil War were held to violate some provision of a state bill of rights. Still, the total number of those decisions was small, probably amounting to no more than twenty in fifteen states over as many as eighty-five years, and they scarcely touched certain fundamental matters such as freedom of speech, freedom of the press, freedom of religion, and freedom of assembly. State bills of rights, whatever may have been their restraining influence as guidelines for public officials, were not heavily litigated documents in the antebellum period. For the defense of liberty, Americans of that time relied less upon enforcing individual rights in court than upon preventing the abuse of public authority through separation of powers, frequent elections, and other such means of republican control.

It remains to be pointed out that early state constitutions, while making fairly detailed provision for the horizontal distribution of power among the legislative, executive, and judicial branches, were generally deficient in prescribing the vertical allocation of power. That is, they did not say very much about the structure of local government and its relation to state authority. Yet Revolutionary America was to a large extent governed in towns, parishes, counties, and municipalities. It was at the local level and by local officials that most laws were enforced, most taxes were levied, and most public services were provided. But since the struggle with Britain did not impinge seriously upon the structure of local government, the first constitution-makers seem to have assumed that the old arrangements would continue and needed little constitutional sanction to do so. In addition, it appears that some framers regarded local government as a subconstitutional matter, properly left to the discretion of the legislature.[85]

Continuity in the South meant retention of the county as the most important unit of local government. The county system had been transplanted to the American continent when Virginia's colonial legislature established eight "shires" in 1634. The number grew slowly at first and then more rapidly. Virginia had 23 counties by 1700, 74 at the end of the Revolution, and 148 on the eve of the Civil War. Georgia erected only 24 before 1800, but added another 108 in the next sixty years. Between 1790 and 1860, the number of counties or equivalent districts in the entire South increased from about 200 to over 1100.[86] This continual creation of new counties, a process that seldom receives any attention in history textbooks, was a very important aspect of American territorial expansion, analogous to the federal government's creation of new territories and admission of new states.

County offices were traditional, dating back in some instances to early medieval England. They included the positions of sheriff, county clerk, justice of the peace, coroner, constable, and surveyor. In Virginia and most of the other southern states existing before 1800, the justices as a group constituted the powerful county court, which combined lawmaking, administrative, and judicial functions into what Jefferson called "the most afflicting of tyrannies."[87] Among other things, this body ordinarily levied county taxes, registered deeds and wills, supervised elections, maintained public buildings, organized slave patrols, licensed taverns, directed the building of roads and bridges, established health regulations, and managed the care of the poor. Nominally appointed by the governor or legislature, the county court tended to be self-perpetuating and to control the appointment of other county officers. With a few exceptions, such as the popular election of sheriffs in Maryland, local government was not directly responsible to the electorate in the eighteenth-century South.[88]

Whereas the Virginia constitution of 1776 treated the county court implicatively as an already-functioning institution, the Arkansas constitution of 1836 formally established a county court system, thereby giving it constitutional status.[89] Similarly, whereas the Mississippi constitution of 1817 left the ordering of local government almost entirely to the legislature (which retained the existing county court system), the constitution of 1832 provided expressly for the election in each county of a five-man governing body to be called the "board of police."[90] The Virginia constitution of 1851 contained five sections under the heading "County Courts" and three more under the heading "County Officers." Even fuller in detail on the subject of local government were the Maryland and Kentucky constitutions framed at about the same time.[91] Along with this growing tendency to constitutionalize basic features of local government, there went a disposition to make local offices elective. In Georgia, it was done partly by statute in 1799 and partly by constitutional amendment in 1812.[92] Popular election of some local officials was written into the Mississippi and Alabama constitutions of 1817 and 1819.[93] But the greatest amount of change took place during a twenty-year period beginning in the early 1830s. By the eve of the Civil War, local government in nearly all southern states had not only come under popular control but acquired more autonomy as a consequence.[94] Intrastate government in nineteenth-century America was arguably decentralized enough to constitute a second tier of federalism in the federal republic.

One of the more obvious general trends in American constitution-making over the years was the lengthening of the average document. For example, Delaware's second constitution, adopted in 1792, proved to be about twice as long as the first, and the third, adopted in 1831, was longer still. Later constitutions usually prescribed the structure and functions of the government in more elaborate detail. They also began to include various instructions and prohibitions designed to set public policy and control the substance of governmental action. The result of this latter trend, which became more pronounced after the Civil War, was a good deal of "superlegislation"—that is, law having statutory quality but constitutional status. Constitutionalization, a strategy employed to serve various purposes, had the effect of lending special legitimacy to a regulation or prohibition and of armoring it against easy repeal whenever power shifted in the state.

Among the instances of superlegislation in southern constitutions one finds clauses forbidding lotteries, clauses providing for election of militia officers, and clauses excluding duellists from public office.[95] There were also clauses regulating divorce. Throughout the entire antebellum period in Alabama, for example, constitutional law allowed a divorce to become final only after a successful suit in chancery and approval by a two-thirds majority of the legislature.[96] Limitation or abolition of imprisonment for debt, though ordinarily accomplished by statute, was written into the constitutions of Alabama (1819) and Maryland (1851).[97] Texas entered the Union in 1845 with a constitution that guaranteed married women the right to retain control of their property, a step already taken in Mississippi by legislative enactment.[98] The Maryland constitution of 1851 fixed the maximum annual interest rate in the state at six percent.[99]

Widespread dissatisfaction with the conduct of state government was manifested in various provisions restricting legislative authority in the realms of public finance, banking, and incorporation. The Texas constitution, for instance, set a limit of $100,000 on state indebtedness, forbade the establishment or renewal of any bank, and required a two-thirds vote of the legislature for the creation of any corporation.[100] The Florida constitution likewise required a two-thirds vote to create a corporation. It authorized banking, but set an absolute limit of twenty years on the life of any bank. Along with many other details, the constitution declared that a bank must have capital stock of at least $100,000 paid in specie, and that a bank's liabilities, including note issues, must at no time exceed double its paid-in capital. It prohibited bank notes in denominations smaller than five dollars, and it limited dividends to ten percent a year.[101] All of this, and much more too, in a charter of fundamental law.

Not much of the economic matter injected into antebellum state constitutions can be labeled conservative. For the most part, says James Willard Hurst, it tended to reflect the liberal politics of the time, expressing "either the liberal's hopes or his disillusioned reading of experience."[102] The main purpose of such superlegislation, if there was one, seems to have been the elimination of special privilege in the relation of government to corporate enterprise. By the time of the Civil War, state constitutional change was becoming a significant avenue of economic reform.

Of course, formal law, and especially constitutional law, is sometimes far removed from social reality. Many of the later southern constitutions contained sections proclaiming the importance of education and making provision for the administration of school lands and school funds. The Louisiana and Texas constitutions of 1845 went further and ordered the establishment of free public schools to be supported by taxation.[103] In Louisiana, the legislature passed a law implementing the mandate, and soon a state superintendent of public education was issuing sanguine reports. Yet progress was actually very slow outside of New Orleans, where local enterprise had already produced a public school program along Massachusetts lines.[104] The rest of Louisiana and the antebellum South as a whole lagged behind other parts of the nation in developing state systems of common schools. No doubt southern resistance to centralized educational reform stemmed primarily from the traditional rural and localistic nature of southern society, but by the 1850's, it had also become an aspect of the sectional conflict over slavery. Northern influences in southern schools aroused increasing resentment and apprehension. In 1859, for instance, Senator James Mason of Virginia warned that imposition of the New England school system on the South would destroy the "peculiar character" of the southern people.[105]

While southern constitutions thus tended to overstate the public commitment to education, they somewhat understated the public commitment to slavery. Five of the fifteen southern states, for a variety of reasons, provided slavery no protection in their constitutions.[106] Beginning with Kentucky in 1792, the other ten eventually did make constitutional provision for the perpetuation of slavery by forbidding the legislature to emancipate slaves without the consent of their owners.[107] But the Kentucky constitution and several others imitating it went on to authorize legislation permitting private manumission, preventing the importation of slaves into the state for sale, and protecting slaves against inhumane treatment.[108] Furthermore, no state constitution *prohibited* private manumission. However, the tenor of statute law was something else again. Legislatures inhibited manumission in a number of ways, such as requiring that liberated slaves leave the state within a specified time and that bond be posted to guarantee such removal. By the 1830s, many states were allowing manumission only through court action or special legislative enactment, and by the eve of the Civil War, some forbade it absolutely.[109] There was an even more striking difference between constitutional law and statute law in the South's response to the antislavery movement. Of the repressive measures passed by many state legislatures to prevent the circulation of abolitionist propaganda there is no suggestion in the antebellum southern constitutions, which continued to proclaim the rights of freedom of speech and freedom of the press.[110]

To some extent, the relative blandness of southern state constitutions with respect to slavery may have reflected the degree of southern consensus on the indefeasibility of the institution. Constitutionalization of state law was a strategy more suitable for dealing with internal dissent than for confronting external danger, and consequently there was little real need to employ it for the protection of slavery in states such as South Carolina and Louisiana. On the other hand, it is perhaps significant that Kentucky, which led the way in erecting a constitutional barrier against legislative emancipation, did so after a fierce struggle between proslavery and antislavery forces in the constitutional convention of 1792.[111] Also, as we have seen, it was in three states with strong localized hostility to slavery (Virginia, North Carolina, and Tennessee) that taxation of slaves became a serious constitutional issue.

Since concern for the protection of slavery was less visible in southern constitutions than in other kinds of southern law, the constitutional history of the antebellum South is less distinctive than its legal history and its political history. Except for South Carolina, which remained essentially oligarchic in its political organization, the slaveholding states participated wholeheartedly in the democratization of American government during the first half of the nineteenth century.[112] Even as the Union began to break apart in 1860, there were greater constitutional differences between eastern and western states than between northern and southern states. This was a paradox with more than one meaning. It exposed a large gap between constitutional forms and social realities in the South, but it also revealed a substratum of consensus in the nation. Study of southern constitutions forcefully reminds one that antebellum southerners were in many ways representative Americans and that much agreement on fundamental values underlay the sectional conflict over slavery, mitigating it at times, but often, strangely enough, only adding aggravation.

Commenting on the constitution of the new state of Mississippi in 1817, a Massachusetts editor declared: "It is . . . so similar to the constitutions of many of the other states, that its perusal does not excite much interest."[113] There is no denying that American constitution-makers after 1787 tended to be more imitative than experimental. For instance, nearly three-fourths of the Kentucky constitution of 1792 was copied from the Pennsylvania constitution of 1790; the Kentucky constitution of 1797 served as the model for the Louisiana constitution of 1812; and the eclectic Tennessee constitution of 1796 borrowed most heavily from the constitutions of Pennsylvania and North Carolina.[114] Yet virtually every new state constitution contained something original (such as Kentucky's extension of constitutional protection to slavery in 1792), and at times the habit of imitation served the spread of innovation (as in the development of an elected judiciary). The cumulative effect in the thirty-four antebellum states was an extraordinary amount of formal constitutional change that contrasts strikingly with the total absence of such change at the national level.

Of course, a written constitution is only the central feature of a functioning constitutional system, which also includes any number of fundamental statutes and judicial rulings, together with certain well-established procedures and customs. Nothing is more illuminating in this respect than the elective process, provided for at length in the typical antebellum state constitution, but dominated by the political party, an institution that had no official constitutional status at all. Although the interplay of party politics and state constitutional development has been only fragmentarily studied, there can be little doubt that partisan motives often shaped the course of constitutional change,[115] and, on the other hand, that constitutional forms significantly influenced party character.[116] Political parties grew up outside the constitutional order, primarily as agencies for selecting candidates and contesting elections. They came to exercise complete control over the nominating phase of the elective process by means of a pyramidal structure of local, state, and national conventions that amounted to a major constitutional innovation. The party system thus functioned in some degree as an informal extension of the constitutional system.

By the middle of the nineteenth century, the convention format was commonplace in the United States, having been adopted as an organizational mode, not only by political parties, but by various interest groups and reform movements. There were, for example, the many southern commercial conventions, the protective tariff and river-and-harbor conventions, the abolitionist, temperance, and women's-rights conventions. Typically a group of citizens called together for a limited period of time to perform a specific service, the convention was an ad hoc form of democracy activated by strong purpose. Decades of experience with constitution-making had accustomed Americans to thinking of the convention as an agency of change. The first constitutional conventions, after all, had been revolutionary bodies dedicated to subverting an old order as well as erecting a new one. In later years, the radical potential of the convention format was sometimes realized in extralegal "reform" conventions, such as those held at Staunton, Virginia, in 1816 and 1825 for the purpose of coercing the state government into calling a regular constitutional convention. The Staunton delegates went no further than memorializing the legislature in somewhat threatening terms, whereas Thomas Dorr and his followers in Rhode Island carried the same tactics to the point of revolution by framing a constitution and attempting to put it into operation in defiance of the existing government.[117]

The quasi-revolutionary character of reform conventions organized to promote constitutional change lent emphasis to the revolutionary possibilities inherent even in a duly authorized constitutional convention itself. Conservatives habitually opposed the calling of constitutional conventions, fearing not only the particular changes being advocated but also the vaguely defined general power of such bodies. According to some theorists, that power had virtually no limits within the boundaries of the state. Thus one convention delegate asserted in 1847: "We are what the people of the State would be, if they were congregated here in one mass meeting. We are what Louis XIV said he was, 'We are the State.' We can trample the constitution under our feet as waste paper, and no one can call us to account save the people."[118] Out of the experience of constitution-making there had developed the idea, especially strong in the South, that the most legitimate embodiment of American sovereignty was a state convention drawn from and acting for the people. The idea colored state constitutional politics, but had its most significant effect on state-federal relations. Southern theories of the nature of the Union were based on the undeniable fact that the Federal Constitution had been merely a recommendation until state conventions installed it as law of the land. It was a state convention, not a state legislature, that ventured to nullify a federal law in 1832. It was a state convention that in 1852 forthrightly proclaimed the right of a state to secede. And it was a train of eleven state conventions that enacted ordinances of secession in 1860 and 1861. State constitutional history from the Revolution to the Civil War is primarily about the erection of permanent structures of government on foundations of fundamental law, but it is also important to note that, in the process, supreme constituent power came to be lodged in ad hoc structures, loosely designed and sporadically erected.

Two

The South and the Federal Constitution

In constitutional terms, the American Revolution was a struggle over the limits of central and local authority within the British Empire. When the conflict between Britain and her colonies came to an end in 1783, the fundamental question at issue was not resolved but merely shifted in its entirety to the American side of the Atlantic. For approximately a century after the birth of the United States, the relation between the central government and the state governments remained the nation's most persistent and intractable constitutional problem, and of course it was a problem made progressively more dangerous by interfusion with the sectional conflict over slavery.

As James Madison explained in *The Federalist*, the Constitution prescribed neither a consolidated national state nor a confederation of sovereign states, but rather a unique combination of both, with two separate systems of government functioning side by side and sharing jurisdiction over the same domain.[1] The powers of the federal government, though supreme wherever appropriately employed, were delegated and enumerated and therefore limited in scope, as well as being subject to a number of specific restrictions. The powers of the state governments were residual and unnamed and therefore of indefinite scope, though likewise subject to a number of specific restrictions. Drawing a line between state and federal authority was one of the fundamental tasks of the framers at Philadelphia. They tried to do it by listing the powers lodged with the central government and by denying many of those same powers and certain others to the states. All other matters of public concern (such as crime and punishment, marriage, inheritance, education, and slavery) fell accordingly within the purview of state authority, as defined and limited by the state constitutions. That was the tacit intent of the framers and the plain meaning of the Tenth Amendment, ratified as part of the Bill of Rights in 1791.

The framers' design of American federalism nevertheless left many important questions unanswered. For one thing, what about those powers delegated to the federal government and *not* expressly denied to the states, such as regulation of naturalization, bankruptcy, and interstate commerce? Could state legislatures engage in concurrent regulation of bankruptcy, or were they excluded by the pre-emptive authority of Congress? Were they excluded even if Congress chose not to legislate on the subject at all? Even more difficult was the problem of ends and means—that is, the relation between powers expressly delegated to Congress and the powers vaguely implied in the necessary-and-proper clause. To use the most obvious illustration, the Constitution did not authorize Congress to grant charters of incorporation, and, in fact, the Constitutional Convention rejected a proposal to do so, thereby acknowledging, it would seem, that such power belonged more properly to state legislatures.[2] Yet Alexander Hamilton, as the first secretary of the treasury, argued with great success in 1791 that Congress had the constitutional authority to incorporate a national bank, not as an end in itself, but as an appropriate means of carrying out the federal government's fiscal responsibilities.[3] Such broad construction of the necessary-and-proper clause, if generally accepted, would obviously convert it into a reservoir of undifferentiated national power, supplementing the powers delegated by enumeration.

Thus the Constitution only sketchily defined the boundary between state and national authority, and it contained no clear provision for the endless work of refining and enforcing the definition. Who, then, would ultimately control the drawing of the line? Who was to decide a contest involving alleged trespass by a state upon the jurisdiction of the United States or vice versa? Who was to determine whether a state had violated one of the prohibitory clauses of the Constitution? And how were such decisions to be made effective? These critical questions defied easy answers and came to be like open wounds that festered instead of healing in the course of time.

The framers of the Constitution depended primarily upon internal checks and balances to prevent misuse of power on the part of the federal government. Unconstitutional legislation would be discouraged in some degree by the bicameral structure of Congress. If any such law were nevertheless enacted, it could be vetoed by the President. If signed into law, it could presumably be nullified by the judiciary. One further possibility was a popular reaction at the polls and consequent repeal of the offending statute.[4] Some of the framers placed their heaviest reliance on judicial review. "The courts of justice," Hamilton wrote in *The Federalist*, "are to be considered as the bulwarks of a limited Constitution against legislative encroachments."[5] But the Convention as a body neither approved nor disapproved the idea that the United States Supreme Court would have the final word on the constitutionality of acts of Congress. There was nothing said in the Constitution about judicial review, and the power could only be inferred, as Hamilton inferred it, from the nature of the instrument and the nature of the judicial process.

The men at Philadelphia were less concerned, however, about possible excesses of the central government than about the probable waywardness of state governments. That, after all, had been much the greater problem under the Articles of Confederation and was one of the major reasons for the calling of the Constitutional Convention. "The State systems are the accursed things which will prevent our being a Nation," wrote General Henry Knox, a New Englander, to one of the framers. "Smite them, in the name of God and the people."[6] In the series of resolutions called the "Virginia Plan," with which the Convention began its work, it was proposed that Congress be given the power "to negative all laws passed by the several States, contravening in the opinion of the National Legislature the articles of Union; and to call forth the force of the Union against any member of the Union failing to fulfill its duty under the articles thereof."[7] The idea of military coercion was soon put aside, but the congressional veto of state laws, which Madison labeled "absolutely necessary," received preliminary approval on May 31, only to be rejected on July 17 and again on August 23, when Charles Pinckney of South Carolina made one last effort to save it.[8] There were several reasons for the rejection, including serious doubts about the practicality of having Congress review all state laws and a strong feeling that the states would never agree to such direct interference in their internal affairs.[9]

Instead, the Convention chose to make restraint of the states a judicial responsibility by means of a clause in Article VI declaring:

> This Constitution and the laws of the United States which shall be made in pursuance thereof; and all treaties made, or which shall be made, under the authority of the United States, shall be the supreme law of the land, and the judges in every State shall be bound thereby, anything in the constitution or laws of any State to the contrary notwithstanding.

The potential range and force of this "supremacy clause" was not wholly apparent to the anti-nationalists with whom it originated. For one thing, the passage could be read as placing reliance principally on *state* judges for protection of the Constitution against violation by their own state governments. But in Article III, the framers provided that the power of the *federal* judiciary should extend to all cases in law and equity arising under the Constitution, laws, and treaties of the United States. This seemed to mean that the Supreme Court would have the authority to review state court decisions involving the federal relationship, and in Section 25 of the Judiciary Act of 1789, Congress expressly invested the Court with such authority.[10] Thus it was in the judicial function that the two systems of government were to be connected and national supremacy secured. State legislatures were not accountable to Congress; state governors were not accountable to the President, but state courts were, in certain crucial ways, accountable to the United States Supreme Court.

The framers, then, apparently intended that differences over the structure of American federalism should be settled primarily by legal rather than political means—the intent being clearer, however, with respect to constitutional limits on state governments than with respect to constitutional limits on the federal government. Judicial resolution had the attraction of seeming more deliberate and impartial and therefore more pacificatory than any political decision was likely to be, but it also had a number of disadvantages. For one thing, not all constitutional issues could be readily transformed into court cases, and for another, there was often a considerable lapse of time between the passage of a law and the final judicial decision on its constitutionality. Moreover, a final judicial decision was not always conclusive. It could be rendered ineffective by failure of the executive branch to provide enforcement or by some other kind of resistance to the court's pronouncement. Consequently, although judges did do much of the work of drawing the line between state and national authority, some controversies were too crucial and/or too aggravated to be resolved in any courtroom. The greatest crises of the Union were acted out in the halls of Congress, and the character of American federalism was ultimately defined on the battlefield.

The Civil War colors our vision of earlier quarrels over the meaning of the Constitution and the structure of the Republic. We are therefore not surprised to learn that the first protests against excessive use of federal power came from the South. In 1790, the legislature of Virginia passed a resolution denouncing Hamilton's proposal for federal assumption of state debts as a measure "repugnant to the Constitution of the United States."[11] Two great Virginians, Thomas Jefferson as secretary of state and James Madison as a leading member of Congress, nevertheless helped secure passage of the assumption bill in order to obtain additional support for locating the new national capital on the banks of the Potomac.[12] At about the same time, a citizen of South Carolina brought suit against the state of Georgia in federal court, and thus initiated the case of *Chisholm v. Georgia*. The Governor of

Georgia vehemently denied that a "sovereign and independent" state could be sued against its will. The Supreme Court, renderings its first decision on a matter of constitutional law, ruled to the contrary in 1793, but that was not the end of the affair. Georgia officials remained unsubmissive, and a bill passed one house of the legislature providing that any federal marshal or other person who attempted to enforce the decision should "suffer death, without the benefit of clergy, by being hanged." Meanwhile, other states had joined in the protest. A constitutional amendment vindicating Georgia's position was passed by Congress and speedily ratified by three-fourths of the states.[13]

Disagreement over the assumption bill was largely a matter of interest rather than constitutional principle, but not of intrinsic sectional interest. For the most part, members of Congress voted according to the size of the debt in their respective states. It happened to be mainly northern states that had the larger debts and therefore stood to gain more from assumption. South Carolina, with a relatively large debt, joined the North in support of the measure.[14] *Chisholm v. Georgia*, although it did raise an important constitutional question, was likewise not particularly a matter of sectional interest. Georgia just happened to be the state that tested the question before the Supreme Court. It might have been New York or Massachusetts instead, for both of those states faced similar suits in federal court.

The first clear-cut sectional division on a major constitutional issue came in 1791 with Hamilton's proposal to charter a Bank of the United States. Such an institution seemed likely to benefit commercial rather than agricultural interests, and the project consequently found little favor among southern congressmen already generally hostile to Hamilton's whole economic program. Madison, retreating from the nationalism that he had espoused in 1787, led the fight against the bill in the House of Representatives, where thirty-three of the thirty-nine votes in its favor came from the northern states and fifteen of the twenty negative votes came from the South.[15] The two Virginians in Washington's cabinet, Jefferson and Attorney General Edmund Randolph, submitted opinions recommending a veto on constitutional grounds, but the President found Hamilton's rebuttal more persuasive and signed the bill into law.[16] In this losing battle, Madison and Jefferson laid down the lines of the standard argument for strict construction that was to become a hallmark of southern constitutional thought. Congress, they maintained, was limited to the powers enumerated in Article I, Section 8, and to whatever additional powers were demonstrably indispensable for carrying the enumerated powers into effect. This narrow conception of the role of the federal government amounted, of course, to a broad conception of the role of state governments, which, as one historian says, "would have rushed in to fill the vacuum" created by the restrictive rule, if it had been adopted.[17]

Along with its economic and sectional aspects, the bank controversy was an early manifestation of the emerging political alignment that would soon develop into the first American party system, with Jefferson and Madison as leaders of the opposition. The running battle between Federalists and Republicans became especially bitter in 1798, when, as war with France seemed imminent, Congress passed the notorious Alien and Sedition Acts. That repressive legislation, though justified by its sponsors as a necessary restraint upon French subversion, was obviously intended to stifle some of the more offensive voices of Republican dissent.[18] Again, as in their fight against the bank, Jefferson and Madison met a political threat with constitutional argument. In the famous Virginia and Kentucky Resolutions, they set forth the classic states-rights theory of the Union—a theory that nullifiers and secessionists would later find eminently serviceable. It began with the assertion that the Constitution was a compact among sovereign states, establishing a general government of strictly limited powers. Acts of that government exceeding those stated limits were, in Jefferson's words, "unauthoritative, void, and of no effect." The Constitution did not make the general government final judge of the extent of its own powers. Instead, each state, as one of the parties to the compact, had an equal right to decide whether there had been an infraction and what to do about it. Concerning redress, Madison spoke only of a state's duty to "interpose for arresting the progress of the evil." Jefferson's draft declared nullification to be the "rightful remedy," and that assertion, although omitted from the text of the resolutions passed by the Kentucky legislature in 1798, was included in a second set of resolutions approved the following year.[19] Thus the states as corporate entities, not the American people, were the creators of the Union, and the states, not Congress or the Supreme Court, were individually the ultimate umpires of the federal system.

The Resolutions were communicated to other state legislatures with requests for their concurrence and cooperation. From nine states to the north of Virginia, all controlled by the Federalists, there came unfavorable responses, many of them declaring that the power to decide on the constitutionality of an act of Congress belonged exclusively to the federal judiciary. The states to the south neither criticized nor supported Virginia and Kentucky but instead simply made no replies at all.[20] Subsequent use of the Resolutions in the sectional conflict has inflated and distorted their contemporary significance. They were eloquent expressions of a widespread hostility to the Alien and Sedition Acts, but their constitutional theory apparently did not reflect majority opinion in the South or in the Republican party. Furthermore, Jefferson and

Madison wrote with the purpose, not of inciting resistance to the central government, but of winning control of that government. The Resolutions were splendid campaign documents for the election of 1800. What followed Jefferson's victory indicated that, for most Americans of that time, states-rights constitutionalism was not so much an abiding faith as a convenient strategy of dissent from the current rulers of national affairs. The strategy seemed to have no consistent partisan or sectional associations; for with Congress and the presidency both in Republican hands, New England Federalists were soon the ones demanding strict construction of the Constitution.

It is well known that Jefferson doubted the constitutionality of the Louisiana Purchase and even drafted an amendment empowering the federal government to acquire territory by treaty.[21] More significant, however, is the fact that few of his political associates agreed with him. Senators John Taylor and Wilson Cary Nicholas of Virginia and Senator John Breckinridge of Kentucky, all of whom had been leading sponsors of the Virginia and Kentucky Resolutions, now looked with disdain upon the narrow view of federal powers expressed by some of their Federalist colleagues.[22] Jefferson himself gradually found it easier to be flexible. As Merrill Peterson says, "The more the President exercised power with righteous purpose the less scrupulous he became toward the abjurations of Republican theory."[23] The Jeffersonian Embargo of 1807–9, with its devastating effect upon New England commerce, completed a striking reversal of constitutional roles. Whereas Virginia a decade earlier had been the center of resistance to the repressive policies of a Massachusetts president, now Massachusetts became the center of resistance to the repressive policies of a Virginia president, and the constitutional arguments coming out of

New England sounded like echoes of the Virginia and Kentucky Resolutions.

Further intensified by the War of 1812, New England disaffection culminated in the convention of twenty-six Federalists that met at Hartford in December 1814. President Madison labeled the gathering a "rebel Parliament," but the delegates, although they did embrace the principles of interposition and nullification, settled rather tamely for recommending a series of amendments to the Constitution.[24] Southern reaction to the rumors of disunionism surrounding the Hartford Convention was well expressed by Thomas Ritchie in his Richmond *Enquirer:* "No man, no association of men, no state or set of states has a right to withdraw itself from the Union of its own accord. The same power which knit us together, can only un-knit. . . . *The majority of states which formed the Union must consent to the withdrawal of any one branch of it.* Until *that* consent has been obtained, any attempt to dissolve the Union, or obstruct the efficiency of its constitutional laws, is *Treason.*"[25]

While Federalist New England was resisting the national authority of a Republican President and Republican Congress, Republican Pennsylvania was resisting the national authority of a Federalist Supreme Court. State officials had already defied the Court several times when, in 1809, Chief Justice John Marshall handed down a decision adverse to Pennsylvania in the case of *United States v. Judge Peters.* Governor Simon Snyder called out the militia, which forcibly prevented the United States marshal from executing the Court's decree. This show of rebellion ended quickly, however, when President Madison informed the Governor that the decree must be enforced. Meanwhile, the legislature had passed a series of resolutions proclaiming itself the guardian of state rights against judicial usurpation and denying that the federal judiciary was an appropriate umpire in state-federal conflicts. Instead, it recommended a constitutional amendment creating "an impartial tribunal" to decide such disputes. Northern and southern states alike rejected the Pennsylvania proposal. The General Assembly of Virginia replied that "a tribunal is already provided by the constitution of the United States, *to wit:* the Supreme Court, more eminently qualified from their habits and duties, from the mode of their selection, and from the tenure of their offices, to decide the disputes aforesaid in an enlightened and impartial manner, than any other tribunal which could be erected."[26] Just a few years later, however, in the case of *Hunter v. Martin*, this sentiment was utterly repudiated by the Virginia Court of Appeals, which adopted the Pennsylvania point of view.[27]

In 1819, Virginia and Pennsylvania both reacted hostilely to *McCulloch v. Maryland*, the decision in which John Marshall upheld the constitutionality of the Second Bank of the United States and laid down a broad definition of the implied powers of Congress. When Pennsylvania proposed a constitutional amendment narrowly restricting congressional authority over banking, the General Assembly of South Carolina responded in a tone of emphatic nationalism. Congress, the legislators formally resolved, was "constitutionally vested with the right to incorporate a bank." Furthermore, they apprehended "no danger" from the powers that the people of the United States had confided to the federal government, believing instead that Congress, in exercising those powers, would "render them subservient to the great purposes of our national compact." That was the voice of South Carolina in 1821.[28]

It seems abundantly clear, then, that during the early decades of the Republic, there was no distinctively southern interpretation of the Constitution and no distinctively southern definition of the nature of the Union. This statement does not signify an intent to take sides in that old debate about when the South came into existence as a conscious sectional entity. Of course there was some sense of southern identity and a southern outlook in national politics from the time of the Revolution onward, but not until some years after the War of 1812 did states-rights constitutionalism come to be identified primarily (though never exclusively) with the South.

To be sure, it can be argued, as Jesse T. Carpenter did in an influential book published many years ago, that the South was a conscious minority from the earliest days of the Republic.[29] But there is much evidence that southerners at the time of the Constitutional Convention expected theirs to become the majority section in the nation. Furthermore, the Jeffersonians of the 1790s seem to have regarded themselves primarily as a political rather than a sectional minority. In a constitutional republic, there are two main lines of action for a minority that considers itself repressed by the majority. It can take a stand as a minority upon its constitutional rights, or it can coalesce with others in an effort to form a new majority and capture control of the government. Jefferson and Madison paid their respects to one of those strategies in the Virginia and Kentucky Resolutions but followed the other one to victory in 1800. For approximately twenty years thereafter, the existence of a Jeffersonian majority in national politics tended to dilute southern distrust of federal power and retard the development of southern sectional consciousness.

By 1820, a transformation of southern attitudes toward the Union had begun, ushering in the antebellum period of American history. The change was first visible in Virginia, which, it should be remembered, had both nationalist and states-rights traditions, exemplified respectively in the Virginia Plan of 1787 and the Virginia Resolutions of 1798. Madison, the principal author of both documents, had reached the middle of his second term as president when the War of 1812 ended. In his last two annual messages to Congress, he sounded more like the Madison of 1787, recommending a strong national defense program, a national bank, a national university, a protective tariff, and federal support for construction of roads and canals. But then, on his last day in office, constitutional scruples led him to veto the "Bonus bill," which would have established a permanent fund for internal improvements.[30] At the time of the veto, a conservative reaction against the postwar nationalism of Congress was already under way in Virginia, where visions of the future were soured by the beginnings of an agricultural depression, soon to be made worse by the Panic of 1819. States-rights feeling was most strongly provoked in Virginia, however, by a cluster of Supreme Court decisions enhancing national authority at state expense, notably *Martin v. Hunter's Lessee* (1816), *Dartmouth College v. Woodward* (1819), *McCulloch v. Maryland* (1819), and *Cohens v. Virginia* (1821). The Martin and Cohens cases were especially provocative because in them Virginia lost a bitter struggle against Supreme Court review of state court decisions.[31]

In South Carolina, the states-rights revolution got started somewhat later and was dramatically illustrated in the changing political behavior of John C. Calhoun. First as a member of Congress and then as secretary of war in the cabinet of James Monroe, Calhoun had the reputation of being one of the foremost nationalists of his day. He favored a standing army, a strong navy, a protective tariff, a national bank, and a program of internal improvements. As the author of the Bonus bill in 1817, he deprecated "refined arguments" about the meaning of the Constitution. "The instrument," he said "was not intended as a thesis for the logician to exercise his ingenuity on. It ought to be construed with plain, good sense."[32] As late as 1823 or 1824, he reportedly declared that the Hamiltonian program of Washington's administration was "the only true policy for the country."[33] But the higher tariff enacted by Congress that same year aroused fierce opposition in South Carolina and enabled the states-rights element to gain the upper hand in state politics. In 1825, the legislature passed resolutions declaring that protective tariffs and internal improvements at federal expense were unconstitutional. Calhoun, already disappointed in his hope of winning the presidency as a nationalist, found that he must either retreat or lose his political standing at home. His mind was also changed by the aggressive attitude of the protectionists, especially as manifested in a tariff convention held at Harrisburg, Pennsylvania, in the summer of 1827. Later that same year he confided to a friend: "After much reflection, it seems to me, that the despotism founded on combined geographical interest, admits of but one effectual remedy, a veto . . . on the part of the States."[34] By the summer of 1828, after Congress passed the "tariff of abominations," he had moved into the states-rights camp and was hard at work writing his famous "Exposition," which the South Carolina legislature subsequently adopted in revised form as official state doctrine, adding a "Protest" against high tariff policy. In the document, Calhoun embraced the principles of strict construction and nullification, arguing that a state had a constitutional right to prevent enforcement within its borders of an unconstitutional federal law.[35]

In its theory of the Union, the Exposition bore considerable resemblance to the Virginia and Kentucky Resolutions, and there are several other interesting similarities worth mentioning. Calhoun in 1828, like Jefferson in 1798, was the

Vice President of the United States, opposing the policies of an Adams administration. In both instances, the documents were written anonymously and with an eye on the approaching presidential election. In both instances, the election ended happily from the authors' point of view, with a President Adams turned out of office and a southerner installed in his place. But the aftermath of victory in 1828 had no parallel in the earlier period. States-rights constitutionalism, which had declined sharply in the South after Jefferson entered the presidency, continued to gain southern converts after the election of Andrew Jackson. In South Carolina, it was soon carried beyond theory to the actual practice of nullification and a resulting head-on confrontation with the Tennessean in the White House. Furthermore, even though southern leadership was generally predominant in the federal government right up to 1860, southerners grew increasingly apprehensive about federal power, and states-rights constitutionalism became an ever more dominant theme in their political rhetoric. Thus the South that turned so emphatically toward the states-rights philosophy in the 1820s seems to have differed significantly from the South of the 1790s in being far more conscious of itself as a permanent and vulnerable minority section.

This change in the southern constitutional outlook reflected a number of circumstances and grievances, such as the growing preponderance of the northern population and an accumulating anger at federal economic policies that seemed inimical to southern agriculture. The crucial event, however, was undoubtedly the great controversy that erupted in 1819 over the admission of Missouri as a slave state. Slavery had been a troublesome issue from time to time in earlier Congresses, but this was the first sectional crisis over the institution. It began with the introduction of the Tallmadge amendment, which, without freeing any of the ten thousand slaves already held in Missouri, would have instituted a program of gradual abolition extending over half a century or more.[36] The amendment met almost unanimous opposition from the southern members of Congress, who thereby gave eloquent testimony to the unity of the South on the subject of slavery. What shocked southerners was the degree of sectional unity displayed for the first time on the other side of the issue. In the House of Representatives, the northern members, most of whom were Republicans, voted almost nine to one for the Tallmadge proposal.[37] To be sure, the amendment was ultimately rejected in favor of a compromise that included the admission of Missouri as a slave state, but in accepting the famous 36° 30' compromise line, the South paid a price that it came to view with deep resentment. Thus, at a critical juncture, the Jeffersonian strategy of majoritarian politics had failed to provide adequate protection for the sectional institution of slavery, and many southerners accordingly began to place more reliance on the Jeffersonian theory of states-rights constitutionalism.

Soon after Missouri entered the Union, South Carolina, the state with the highest percentage of slaves in its population, and the state that had been the most affected emotionally by the black revolution of the 1790s in Haiti, experienced its own biggest racial scare when the Denmark Vesey conspiracy was uncovered. The execution of some thirty-five Negroes, even though no violence had been committed, indicated the level of apprehension in the state. Many South Carolinians no doubt agreed with the assertion of the pamphleteer Robert J. Turnbull that the Vesey plot was one of the "choicest fruits" of the Missouri controversy because the debates in Congress had inspired slaves with false hopes of freedom.[38] Two other slave disturbances troubled South Carolina during the 1820s, and then, in 1831, came the bloody Nat Turner uprising in Virginia. By that time, William Lloyd

Garrison had founded *The Liberator* in Boston, inaugurating a new and more aggressive phase of the antislavery crusade. Uneasiness about the future security of slavery mingled with South Carolinian anger over the protective tariff and probably intensified the belligerence with which the state pursued nullification in 1832–33.[39] Nor should it be forgotten that shortly after the Nullification crisis came to an end, Parliament passed an act abolishing slavery in the British West Indies, thereby contributing to the South's sense of isolation in an increasingly hostile world.

From the Nullification struggle until his death in 1850, Calhoun took the lead in enunciating and elaborating the theory of the Union that is commonly associated with the antebellum South. His argument started from the assumption that sovereignty was indivisible and had been retained by the people of the states in their corporate capacities. It was the independent and sovereign states, then, that had by mutual agreement produced the Constitution, creating the federal government as their "common agent" charged with a limited number of responsibilities and invested only with the power needed to carry them out. Since an agent obviously did not have the last word in a disagreement between itself and one of its principals, the Constitution could not be interpreted as empowering the Supreme Court to review state court decisions, the Judiciary Act of 1789 to the contrary notwithstanding. Instead, the final decision in a dispute between the federal government and a state rested with the people of the state acting through a convention. Such a convention, representing ultimate sovereign authority, could nullify an unconstitutional federal action by forbidding its enforcement within the jurisdiction of the state. As a last resort, the convention could even cut the state's ties with the rest of the Union and restore it to complete independence.[40]

Although Calhoun affirmed the right of a state to secede and regarded secession as a course of action that might one day become necessary, he gave it only a marginal place in his political design. His goal was not southern independence but southern security within the Federal Union. By midcentury, some southerners were really aiming at disunion, and for many others the *threat* of disunion had become a potent weapon in the sectional conflict. The South throughout the following decade was always much closer to unity on the constitutional right of secession than on the practical wisdom of seceding at a particular moment. As for nullification, the doctrine itself won only limited support outside of South Carolina during the crisis of 1832–33, although Andrew Jackson's belligerent defense of national supremacy did broaden southern sympathy for the nullifiers.[41] From one southern state capital after another came resolutions reaffirming opposition to the protective tariff but disapproving of the action taken by South Carolina. The Alabama legislature, for example, declared that nullification was "unsound in theory and dangerous in practice," and the Georgia legislature denounced it as an unconstitutional remedy that would tend to promote "civil commotion and disunion."[42] Strangely enough, Georgia officials at that very time were defying a Supreme Court decision upholding the rights of the Cherokee Indians.[43] Such action amounted to an unceremonious form of interposition, and there were other instances of antebellum southern resistance to federal authority, but nullification in its full formal dress was never a part of southern strategy after 1833. At all events, nullification and other kinds of interposition were of limited use to the South in the slavery conflict because the matters chiefly at issue lay beyond the jurisdiction of the southern states.

In developing a theoretical foundation for the defense of

slavery within the Union, Calhoun therefore came to rely less upon the doctrine of state sovereignty, with its corollaries, nullification and secession, than he did upon the principle of the "concurrent majority."[44] Rejecting rule by the numerical majority as a form of tyranny, he argued that a true constitutional majority was a concurrence of the primary interest groups in a society. In the context of antebellum America, this meant a government so arranged that decisions would be made by concurring sectional majorities, with each section thus having a veto on the proposals of the other.[45] It was an idea as old as the Constitution. Madison in the Convention of 1787 casually suggested that representation be apportioned differently in the two houses of Congress so that "the Southern Scale would have the advantage in one House, and the Northern in the other."[46] Another delegate argued in favor of a plural executive that would include representatives of the several sections.[47] Calhoun, near the end of his life, proposed the establishment of a dual presidency, and that scheme was revived by several southern leaders during the secession crisis of 1860–61. One variation brought forward by Andrew Johnson, would have required that the presidency alternate every four years between free and slaveholding states.[48] But when it came to actual practice, the principle of the concurrent majority resided mainly in Congress, where the Senate often curbed stronger antislavery tendencies in the House of Representatives. It was senatorial opposition, for example that prevented passage of the Tallmadge amendment in 1819 and the Wilmot Proviso in 1846. Of course that is why southerners fought so bitterly in 1850 against the admission of California and the consequent termination of sectional equality in the Senate, which a Charleston quarterly called "the last, the best, the strongest guarantee" of southern security.[49] As a matter of fact, however, the Senate continued to be a proslavery stronghold throughout the 1850s.

Negative power, whether in the invocation of states-rights constitutionalism or in the operation of a concurrent majority, could not provide all the protection that slavery needed. Certain problems, such as the recovery of fugitive slaves, called for positive action by the federal government. Furthermore, many southerners could never have been satisfied with the reactive role of a permanent minority excluded from the inner circles of policy-making. "We are the land of rulers," declared the Mayor of Savannah in January 1861.[50] The Missouri crisis made southerners more distrustful of national power, but it did not reduce their desire to determine national policy. Throughout the antebellum period, the deepening southern devotion to states-rights constitutionalism was accompanied, and to some extent contradicted, by a continuing southern investment in majoritarian political strategy. A South Carolina secessionist surveying the alternatives in 1856 declared that he favored creation of "a Southern party which would either succeed and thus govern the country or fail and thus form a compact Southern party ready for action."[51] The strains resulting from this dual strategy were all the more severe because of the extent to which the South succeeded in controlling the operation of the federal government.

Alexander H. Stephens, one of those who suffered acutely from the strain of conflicting loyalties to state and nation, reminded his fellow Georgians in 1861 that southerners had outnumbered northerners in the presidency, the executive departments, the foreign service, the presidency *pro tem* of the Senate, the speakership of the House, the Supreme Court, the higher military echelons, and the federal bureaucracy. "With but few exceptions, he said, the South has controlled the Government in its every important action from the beginning."[52] The fundamental reason for this remarkable ascendancy of a minority section was that southerners were usually the majority in the majority party—first the Jeffersonian Republicans and then the Jacksonian Democrats. Furthermore, in any conflict over slavery, southerners were always more united than northerners, and their moral disadvantage could be offset by invoking the Constitution, by arousing fears of disunion, and by exploiting the racial feelings common to both sections.[53] The South also profited from the "doughface" factor in American politics, by which I mean the circumstance that, until the advent of the Republican party in the 1850s, every northerner seriously aspiring to high office in the federal government had to come to terms with slavery.

The predominance of southerners in the federal government and the location of the national capital on southern ground produced an environment in which slavery was normal and respectable, and its critics were disreputable and subversive. No prominent antislavery leader was appointed to high federal office before Lincoln's administration. At the same time, no southerner was too extreme in his proslavery views to be ineligible for such an honor. In 1844, Calhoun became secretary of state with the unanimous approval of the Senate.[54] As late as 1858, Robert Barnwell Rhett, one of the foremost disunionists in the country, was seeking a federal job for one of his business associates.[55] In the summer of 1860, when many threats of disunion were punctuating the presidential campaign, the South Carolina secessionist William B. Trescot was appointed assistant secretary of state, just in time to act as an intermediary for his state during the crisis that followed Lincoln's election.[56] A proslavery attitude consistently prevailed in the conduct of foreign relations no matter who occupied the White House. It was during the administration of John Quincy Adams, for instance, that the most strenuous efforts were made to secure treaties providing for the return of fugitive slaves from Canada and Mexico. By 1860, the principal sectional issues, such as the tariff, national banking, internal improvements, and slavery in the territories, had all been resolved in favor of the South as far as official national policies were concerned. It was a part of sectional strategy for southerners to complain of a northern bias in the federal government, but there were moments of candor when they could not refrain from expressions of pride in the fact that it had been peculiarly *their* government. "It is written on the brightest page of human history," said James H. Hammond of South Carolina on the floor of the Senate in 1858, "that we, the slaveholders of the South, took our country in her infancy; and, after ruling her for sixty out of the seventy years of her existence, we shall surrender her to you without a stain upon her honor, boundless in prosperity, incalculable in her strength, the wonder and the admiration of the world."[57]

Those who control the operations of the federal government shape the applicative meaning of the Constitution. By 1860, southern influence had made the document more of a bulwark for slavery than its framers ever intended. A few northern members of Congress might continue to insist that the Constitution treated slaves only as persons and not as property, but seven decades of consistent government practice indicated otherwise. Although Congress was authorized "to exercise exclusive legislation in all cases whatsoever" over the District of Columbia, southerners had convinced themselves and many northerners that abolition of slavery in the District would be illegal without the consent of Virginia and Maryland. The fugitive-slave clause had been construed broadly as empowering Congress to enact implemental legislation without regard for the rights of free blacks, whose liberties the legislation threatened. More than that, the Supreme Court had given the clause a special status by endorsing the myth that it "constituted a fundamental article, without the adoption of which the Union could not have been formed."[58] In the Dred Scott decision of 1857, the clause authorizing Congress to "make all needful rules and regulations" respecting federal territory had been construed narrowly as including no power to prohibit slavery. This meant that southerners were at last authoritatively vindicated in their complaint that the Missouri Compromise restriction was unconstitutional. The decision had the effect of confirming slavery as a national institution, incontestably legal wherever it was not forbidden by state law. The only power possessed by Congress with respect to slavery, said Chief Justice Roger B. Taney, was "the power coupled with the duty of guarding and protecting the owner in his rights."[59]

It is easy to understand the mixed feelings of many southerners in the winter of 1860–61 as they contemplated separating themselves from the structure of government that bore so many marks of southern influence. But the structure had always been fragile, and the majoritarian strategy had been breaking down ever since passage of the Kansas-Nebraska Act in 1854. To southerners, the Republican victory in 1860 meant that abolitionism was now ascendant in the North and would soon place its stamp of possession upon the federal government, its gloss of interpretation upon the Constitution. The election of Lincoln therefore became the signal for pursuing the logic of states-rights constitutionalism to its ultimate conclusion.

Three

The Confederacy as a Constitutional System

John M. Daniel, a grandnephew of Supreme Court Justice Peter V. Daniel, returned home from a diplomatic post during the secession winter of 1860–61 and resumed his editorship of the Richmond *Examiner*. Although his appointment abroad had come from Franklin Pierce, he hated Yankees with a passion that inflamed his editorial prose. Northerners, according to Daniel, were "a people lost to all shame . . . cowards by nature, thieves upon principle, and assassins at heart." They were a race of creatures "abounding in the stenches of moral decomposition." They were vermin swarming in a dunghill. "The tiger that laps the blood," he wrote, "and the beetle that gorges excrement, are but Yankees of the animal kingdom . . . our feelings towards [these] scarabaei and vipers of humanity should be characterized neither by rage nor nausea, but by a fixed cheerful Christian determination to . . . curb their inordinate and bloody lusts by such adequate means as natural wit suggests; and, as a general thing, to kill them wherever we find them, without idle questions as to whether they are reptiles or vermin."[1]

Nothing angered Daniel more than the moral isolation of the Confederacy as a result of northern antislavery propaganda. "We have not a friend on earth," he declared. "We have become the stock monsters of all public showmen; the wickedness of Southern slaveholders is received as the first axiom of political truth . . . Our position before the world, during the last ten years of the Union, has been thoroughly and perfectly odious . . . because we were, till lately, bound to another people, who hated us, and, when not too busy in cheating us, made our injury and defamation the business of their existence." An *Examiner* editorial appearing in August 1864 urged that a presidential message be sent round the world denying the northern falsehood that secession was but a means to an ignoble end, that the South "had no higher or nobler cause to fight for than the possession of a certain quantity of serviceable negro flesh." The direct reverse was true, Daniel insisted. "The question of slavery is only one of the minor issues; and the cause of the war, the whole cause, on our part, is the maintenance of the sovereign independence of these States." But three months later, when Jefferson Davis proposed the enlistment of forty thousand slaves, with emancipation offered as the reward for faithful service, Daniel objected strenuously. This would be a first step toward universal abolition and thus a moral surrender to northern principles, he said. "It would be a confession, not only of weakness, but of absolute inability to secure the object for which we undertook the war."[2]

Daniel's inconsistency can be viewed as exemplifying a confusion among southerners about what they were fighting for, but it may have been just loose phrasing—a journalistic slip of the pen. If, instead of saying "the object for which we undertook *the war*," Daniel had said, "the object for which we undertook *secession*," he would have been much less self-contradictory. Secession was the ultimate response to northern attacks on slavery, but the war was a defense of the right to secede and form an independent nation.

In recent years, southern commitment to separate nationhood has been depreciated by some historians. Kenneth M. Stampp, for instance, calls southern nationalism "the most flimsy and ephemeral of dreams."[3] The authors of *Why the South Lost the Civil War* likewise deny that southerners were imbued in any significant degree with a spirit of national purpose. "We believe," they say, "that the Confederacy functioned as a nation only in a technical, organizational sense, and not in a mystical or spiritual sense. . . . Confederate nationalists surely existed, but Confederate nationalism was more a dream than anything else."[4] On the other hand, Emory M. Thomas maintains that the unique social economy of the Old South combined with certain distinctive cultural traits to produce a "nascent" southern nationalism that then matured during the hard experience of war. By 1865, he writes, the Confederate struggle had no other goal than "independence, the ability to exist as a people." The ceremony at Appomattox therefore truly marked the "Death of a Nation."[5] David M. Potter thought that antebellum expressions of southern nationalism were "born of resentment and not of a sense of separate cultural identity." But out of "the shared sacrifices, the shared efforts, and the shared defeat . . . of the Civil War," he added, there arose a "deeply felt" southern nationalism that "flourished in the cult of the Lost Cause."[6] It seems to me that the quality of southern nationalism at the beginning of the Civil War compares not unfavorably with the quality of American nationalism in the early days of the Revolution. In both instances, the primary bonding element at first was a common hostility to the alleged oppressor; in both instances, the desire for independence was widespread but far from universal; in both instances, the sense of national identity drew added strength—for a time, at least—from the ordeal of conflict. One important difference was that southerners in 1861 were more severely torn by conflicting feelings, especially by their deep affection for the old Federal

Union and their hatred of northern abolitionism. Perhaps the critical difference, however, is the effect of hindsight on historical judgment. "We have lost," writes Steven A. Channing, "the sense of contingency, of possibility inherent in the course of events as they unraveled."[7] Thus, victory in 1783 made the Declaration of Independence a reality; defeat in 1865 turned the idea of southern nationhood, as it flourished in 1861, into an empty dream.

Although the number of antebellum southerners wholeheartedly dedicated to the achievement of independence was probably not very large, many others were tempted by the idea and partly converted—ambivalent about disunion but ready to be swept up in the great secessionist impulse after Lincoln's election. One thing enhancing southern nationalism in the winter of 1860–61, was a reasonable expectation of success. If southerners were divided about the wisdom of immediate secession, northerners were not only divided but badly confused in their response to the secession of the lower South. With the future of the upper South hanging in the balance, with most northern Democrats and more than a few Republicans in favor of allowing the seceding states to depart in peace, with Mayor Fernando Wood even proposing to make New York a free city, it seemed unlikely that the incoming Republican administration could mount an effective effort at coerced reunification. Many southern leaders half-convinced themselves for a time that the North would acquiesce in peaceable separation. Robert Toombs is said to have told his fellow Georgians that he stood ready to drink all the blood likely to be shed in the crisis.[8] Such hopes were encouraged by the utterances of northern Democrats like Congressman Daniel Sickles, later a major general in the Union Army, who declared in December 1860: "No man will ever pass the boundaries of the city of New York for the purpose of waging war against any State of this Union."[9] There was some talk that civil war, if it came, might be fought primarily in northern streets between the enemies and friends of the South. Franklin Pierce, had already predicted just such a conflict in a letter to Jefferson Davis, and during the early months of 1861, the Richmond *Enquirer* repeatedly encouraged its readers to hope for a revolution in the North that would disable the Republicans as a threat to the South.[10]

Civil war, peaceable separation, a prolonged period of confrontation without actual conflict, perhaps even a negotiated reconstruction of the Union—all of these seemed to be alternative possibilities in February 1861, when delegates from the seceded states met at Montgomery, Alabama, to establish a new federal republic. Their purposeful demeanor contrasted sharply with the uncertainty reigning elsewhere in the country, as they boldly assumed the multiple role of provisional congress, electoral college, and constitutional convention. "It was," says one historian, "the most powerful body, constitutionally speaking, ever assembled in the history of Anglo-American institutional development."[11] The convention took less than a week to adopt a provisional constitution and elect a president and vice president. A twelve-man committee appointed to draft a permanent constitution finished its task on February 28. The delegates then debated the text clause by clause, making numerous revisions and approving the constitution in its final form on March 11, just one week after Abraham Lincoln took the oath of office in Washington.[12] The document is especially valuable as a testament of Confederate national purpose because it was written after the commitment of the lower South to independence but before the exigencies of war had made constitutionalism itself a luxury that could scarcely be afforded.

Back in November, Senator James H. Hammond of South

Carolina had written that the seceding states "should at once adopt the present Federal Constitution without any modification," adding that he foresaw "the most terrible results" from any attempt to improve upon it.[13] Hammond's wishes were substantially realized in the Constitution framed at Montgomery. "We have changed the constituent parts, but not the system of government," said Jefferson Davis in his inaugural address. "The Constitution framed by our fathers is that of these Confederate States."[14] Historians who belittle southern nationalism point to this resemblance as further proof of their case, but constitutional originality is hardly a reliable measure of national spirit. Antebellum southerners had rarely expressed anything but reverence for the Constitution of 1787, properly construed. Secession was in their eyes an effort to preserve the true American constitutional system by dissolving the Federal Union and reconstituting a smaller version freed from the malign influence of northern commercialism and abolitionism. One may, to be sure, raise the technical question of whether separatism aimed at preservation of a threatened status quo can appropriately be classified as a variety of nationalism. Nevertheless, the text of the Confederate Constitution, like the casualty record of the Confederate Army, seems to be *prima facie* evidence of strong dedication to the idea of an independent southern nation.

Despite its generally derivative character, the Constitution contained a number of deviations from the original model, some of which reaffirmed and validated southern constitutional doctrines hammered out during the sectional conflict. For one thing, it forbade Congress to pass any law "denying or impairing the right of property in negro slaves," and it required congressional protection of slavery in any territories that might be acquired. Thus the central purpose of secession was achieved by the forthright establishment of a slaveholding republic. At the same time, the Constitution formally installed the principle of state sovereignty. To Congress, powers were "delegated" instead of "granted," and the preamble was revised to begin as follows: "We, the people of the Confederate States, each State acting in its sovereign and independent character . . . " The Constitution omitted the controversial "general welfare" clause, which Hamilton and others had used to justify a broadening of federal authority. It also prohibited protective tariffs and severely restricted expenditure of federal money for internal improvements. In addition, it transferred the power of initiating constitutional amendments to the states, excluding Congress from the process altogether, and it made a Confederate official liable to impeachment, not only by the national House of Representatives, but also by the legislature of the state in which he lived and worked.[15]

Yet the truly striking feature of this constitution written and adopted by representatives of the deep South is not the extent to which it incorporated states-rights doctrines, but rather the extent to which it transcended those principles in order to build a nation. The preamble stated that the purpose of the document was "to form a permanent federal government," and nowhere in its text did the framers assert or imply that this government was to be the mere agent of the states. Neither did they eliminate the national supremacy clause, or the necessary-and-proper clause, and, contrary to the wishes of some delegates, they provided no basis for nullification and included no acknowledgment of a right of secession.[16] The Constitution did place some new limitations upon all three branches of the central government, but it retained the essential elements of vigorous nationality. Confederate nationalism, soon to be stimulated by the centralizing pressures of war, was written into the Confederate Constitution by men committed to the principles of states rights but addicted, in many instances, to the exercise of national power.

From the standpoint of political science, the most interesting components of the Confederate Constitution are various innovations more or less unrelated to the sectional conflict.[17] These were essentially technical changes, some minor and some major, reflecting seven decades of experience with the operation of the American government. For example, claims against the United States had always been handled by private legislation that placed an increasingly heavy burden on Congress. A so-called "Court of Claims" established in 1855 had only recommendatory powers and was therefore not really a judicial body. The Confederate Constitution specifically directed Congress to create a judicial tribunal for the disposal of claims against the government.

Corresponding with a general trend in nineteenth-century constitutional development at the state level, the Confederate Constitution strengthened the executive at the expense of the legislature. It required a two-thirds vote of both houses for appropriations other than those formally requested by the president. In addition, the president was empowered to "approve any appropriation and disapprove any other appropriation in the same bill." This so-called "item veto," already adopted by the new state of Kansas, became a common feature in state constitutions after the Civil War. Executive participation in the legislative process was also encouraged by a clause authorizing Congress to grant each department head a seat on the floor of either house, together with the privilege of discussing measures relevant to his duties.

The marked increase in executive control over appropriations was accompanied by a sharp reduction of executive patronage. The Constitution authorized the president to remove department heads and members of the diplomatic corps at pleasure, but other civil officers of the executive department could be dismissed only for cause, such as dishonesty, inefficiency, or neglect of duty. This provision, substituting clarity for the uncertainty of the United States Constitution on the subject, struck a heavy blow at the spoils system and the support that it gave to political parties. In another move to separate the executive from party politics, the framers of the Constitution added their boldest innovation by limiting presidential tenure to a single term of six years. Presumably, a president ineligible to succeed himself would be more disposed to serve the whole people and place the national interest above partisan considerations. Just such a change in the United States Constitution has been proposed many times on the floor of Congress.[18]

How does one explain the aversion to party politics embodied in the Confederate Constitution? After all, it was through the operation of the party system that the South had for many years exercised more political power than its population warranted. But of course that advantage had turned sour with the emergence of an aggressive northern party devoted to antislavery principles. No doubt the election of Lincoln was enough in itself to inspire a revulsion against party politics in the slaveholding states. At the same time, the framers of the Constitution were especially sensitive about political corruption because of recent scandals that had tainted the administration of James Buchanan and embarrassed the southerners closely associated with it.[19]

In an important essay on the Confederate Constitution, Donald Nieman has argued persuasively that the innovations related to the presidency reflected the persisting influence of eighteenth-century republican ideology in mid-nineteenth-century America.[20] The founders of the Confederacy were naturally well aware of their resemblance to the founding fathers of 1776 and 1787. No coincidence could have been more appropriate than their election of a president named after Thomas Jefferson and a vice president named after Alexander Hamilton. It was accordingly altogether natural that such men, in drafting the fundamental law of their new nation, should have sought to nourish the old republican ideals of civic virtue and chaste government, while discouraging the excesses of partisanship and patronage. Thus the Confederate reconstruction of the American presidency was nostalgic as well as progressive. Indeed, the constitution-makers at Montgomery seem to have regarded themselves as both conservators and innovators—that is, as defenders of traditional rights who had been forced to become revolutionaries and builders of a new political order. The innovations in the Confederate Constitution therefore reflect not only the principles of republicanism but the aspirations of nationhood. This is especially true of those provisions manifesting a hostility to party politics. Renunciation of partisanship in the antebellum South was associated with the efforts of John C. Calhoun and others to promote southern unity. In that context, it was an expression not so much of classic republicanism as of rudimentary southern nationalism. The mixture of reverent imitation and bold invention in the Confederate Constitution suggests an ambivalent desire to be quintessentially American and at the same time distinctively, independently southern.

It took just six weeks for conventions in the seven Confederate states to ratify the Constitution. More than ninety-five percent of the delegates voted to do so. Only in South Carolina was there a significant amount of dissatisfaction with the document, particularly because of its failure to prohibit the admission of nonslaveholding states to the Confederacy, and its retention of the three-fifths compromise in the apportionment of representation. Yet even the South Carolina convention, after some heated debate, finally approved ratification by a vote of 138 to 21.[21] The attack on Fort Sumter in April put an end to the hope for peaceable dissolution of the Union and brought four more states into the Confederacy. Conventions in Virginia, North Carolina, and Arkansas, after having passed ordinances of secession, ratified the Confederate Constitution in June. Tennessee became the only state to submit the Constitution to its electorate, which on August 1 voted almost three to one in favor of ratification.[22] Later, secessionist elements in Kentucky and Missouri gained somewhat dubious admission to the Confederacy. That made it nominally a republic of thirteen states, just like the new nation of 1776. Military conditions soon reduced both Kentucky and Missouri to mere shadow membership, and neither state ever properly ratified the Confederate Constitution. Nevertheless, their irregularly chosen senators and representatives continued to sit in the Confederate Congress until the end of its days.[23]

———

By the summer of 1861, the Confederacy extended from Chesapeake Bay to the Rio Grande, embracing an area about four-fifths the size of the original United States. It was an unfledged nation, still organizing itself, and also a nation at war with a more powerful enemy, facing attack along several thousand miles of borderland and coastline. The war profoundly influenced the development of the Confederacy as a political entity and in the end destroyed it, but not before an interesting new chapter had been written in the history of constitutional government.

The delegates at Montgomery had ably performed their duty as founding fathers by designing a structure of government, investing it with power, and placing limits on that power. But a constitution is just paper until its words are translated into a functioning constitutional system. For approximately a year, the Confederacy operated under its provisional constitution, with a provisional Congress (essentially the Montgomery convention augmented after the Fort Sumter hostilities by representation from the upper South), and a provisional president chosen by Congress. It was this temporary government that created the executive departments, moved the capital from Montgomery to Richmond, sent diplomatic agents to Europe, organized the military forces, and directed the early prosecution of the war. The first national elections were held in November 1861. That was a time of bright prospects for the Confederacy, but the outlook had changed three months later when the permanent constitutional system was at last installed. Fort Henry and Fort Donelson had just fallen, and Nashville would have to be evacuated as a consequence.[24] The South had begun to lose the war where the war was going to be lost—in the Mississippi Valley. Jefferson Davis, who had been re-elected to serve a regular six-year term as president, took the oath of office on February 22 in the midst of a winter downpour. "At the darkest hour of our struggle," he said in his inaugural address, "the Provisional gives place to the Permanent Government." He nevertheless found many reasons for hope and pride, including the constitutional record of the Confederacy in its first year. "Through all the necessities of an unequal struggle," he asserted, "there has been no act on our part to impair personal liberty or the freedom of speech, of thought, or of the press. The courts have been open, the judicial functions fully executed, and every right of the peaceful citizen maintained as securely as if a war of invasion had not disturbed the land."[25]

Yet in one important respect, the judicial system was defective, and the design of the new republic remained unfulfilled. In the constitutional history of the Confederacy there is no stranger chapter than the one we might title: "A Supreme Court That Never Was." The provisional constitution, adopted by the Montgomery convention in February 1861, authorized one district court for each state and provided that the district judges assembled should constitute the Supreme Court. In March, the same body of men sitting as the provisional Congress passed legislation establishing a judicial system in line with the constitutional mandate. Surprisingly, the act vested the Supreme Court with broader power to review state court decisions than had been conferred upon the Supreme Court of the United States by the Judiciary Act of 1789. Ardent states-righters were appalled by this capitulation to the spirit of John Marshall, and in addition, the impracticability of having district judges double as members of the Supreme Court soon became obvious. Therefore, in July 1861, Congress voted to suspend the sitting of the Supreme Court until it could be organized under the permanent Constitution.[26]

In his first message to the first permanent Congress on February 25, 1862, Davis reminded its members of their constitutional duty to establish a Supreme Court.[27] Bills to that purpose were introduced in both houses but not acted upon before adjournment, and the same thing happened in the second session, running from August to October.[28] As the year 1863 dawned with nothing having been done, Attorney General Thomas Hill Watts, in a report to the President, complained of many conflicting court decisions awaiting appellate disposition, which he said, demonstrated "the necessity for prompt action on the part of Congress." Then he added: "Uniformity in the construction of statutes, the preservation of constitutional landmarks, and justice to the property and person of the citizen, all call for the establishment of the

Supreme Court."[29] Soon after Congress reconvened on January 12, Senator Benjamin H. Hill of Georgia introduced a bill that set off two months of debate on the issue. There were some senators who wanted no Supreme Court at all, but the principal conflict was over an amendment, offered by Clement C. Clay of Alabama, stripping the Court of the power to review state court decisions. At one point in the struggle, Hill traded insults with the Alabama hotspur, William Lowndes Yancey, becoming so incensed that he bounced an inkwell off Yancey's head. The Senate finally approved the amendment, passed the bill, and sent it to the House of Representatives. There, the judiciary committee recommended passage with the controversial amendment deleted, but the House as a whole voted to postpone the measure until the next session.[30] In the fourth and final session of the First Congress extending from December 1863 to February 1864, the Supreme Court bill was postponed once more by the House, and then apparently forgotten. Further efforts likewise came to naught. As late as March 1865, with Grant's army hammering away at the defenses of Richmond, the House voted to table a bill organizing the Supreme Court.[31]

The struggle over the Court pointed up the fact that antebellum southern nationalism (in the sense of wanting independence from the North) converted readily into Confederate anti-nationalism (in the sense of opposing a strong central government). Traditional fear of a national judiciary as a threat to state sovereignty undoubtedly had much to do with the failure of Congress to carry out one of the major provisions of the Confederate Constitution. But there were additional reasons for the delinquency. The opposition of some members was an expression of hostility to Jefferson Davis and to the kind of men he would probably select for service on the Court. For instance, a suspicion that he might appoint Judah

P. Benjamin or John A. Campbell as Chief Justice may have influenced a number of votes.³² Furthermore, in the worsening military situation, the question of organizing the Supreme Court came to seem less than urgent and at the same time too controversial for resolution by a nation fighting desperately to survive.

The lack of a Supreme Court accounts in part for the diffuse and desultory character of Confederate constitutional history. There being no single authoritative voice, judicial interpretation of the Constitution was scattered among the various state courts and Confederate district courts. This circumstance tended to increase the significance of constitutional discussion in Congress and constitutional pronouncements from the executive branch, such as certain veto messages of the President and certain opinions of the Attorney General.

Jefferson Davis returned thirty-three acts of Congress without his signature, far more than any American president down to that time, and he justified eleven of those vetoes on constitutional grounds.³³ In some instances, his objections were merely technical, but in others there were major issues at stake. For instance, he vetoed one bill providing for a "Veteran Soldiers' Home," pointing out that its effect was to confer corporate powers on the board of managers, something that Congress had no constitutional authority to do. In language reminiscent of Jefferson's quarrel with Hamilton over the Bank of the United States, Davis declared: "The whole history and theory of the contest in which we are engaged and the express recognition in our Constitution of the sovereignty of the States preclude all idea of so widely extending by construction the field of implied powers."³⁴

Although the provisional Congress, in organizing the executive branch of the government, was generally disposed to follow the United States model, it omitted a department of the interior and expanded the office of attorney general into a department of justice. As a consequence, the Confederate attorney general acquired several administrative responsibilities that in the United States belonged to the secretary of the interior, including supervision of the bureau of public printing and the bureau of patents. But his primary duty remained the equivalent of what it had been in American government since 1789, namely: "to prosecute and conduct all suits in the Supreme Court, in which the Confederate States shall be concerned, and to give his advice and opinion upon questions of law, when required by the President of the Confederate States, or when requested by any of the heads of departments, touching any matters that may concern their departments on subjects before them."[35] Beginning with Judah P. Benjamin, four men served as attorney general of the Confederacy, and a fifth held the post *ad interim* for about two months.[36] Of course there were never any Supreme Court cases to handle, but the official opinions of the attorneys general, which fill a sizable volume, had considerable influence on the conduct of the government and dealt not infrequently with constitutional issues. Technically, an opinion was advisory, rather than conclusive, but Davis insisted that the advice, when requested, ought to be followed as a matter of interdepartmental comity.[37]

One of the anomalies of the Civil War was the extent to which the Confederacy, in the midst of political disruption and armed conflict, sustained a legal continuity with the United States. The Montgomery convention not only adopted a revised version of the American Constitution but also declared that the laws of the United States in effect on November 1, 1860, insofar as they were applicable, should become the laws of the Confederacy.[38] More than that, the whole body of American constitutional interpretation and judicial precedent was carried over into Confederate law. Attorney General Watts declared in one of his opinions: "Such clauses of the United States Constitution, as are incorporated, without alteration or change, into the Confederate Constitution, must have been adopted with full knowledge of the established and uniform construction given them in the United States, and such construction thus becomes a part of our Constitution."[39] Confederate judges—even state judges—cited the decisions of John Marshall with surprising frequency. According to the Alabama historian Albert Burton Moore, "It would be difficult for a reader of Southern judicial literature to discover that there had been a withdrawal from the Union."[40]

Cases pending in southern federal courts at the time of secession were continued in Confederate district courts. "So smooth was the transition," says William M. Robinson, Jr., in *Justice in Grey*, "that writs issued by United States authority were returned to Confederate courts and the judgments were executed by Confederate marshals. Indictments returned by United States grand juries were tried by Confederate petit juries, and persons convicted of offenses against the United States were imprisoned at Confederate expense."[41] However, Attorney General Watts used his influence to discourage continuity in the enforcement of criminal law. For example, he advised the Postmaster General that a postal employee in South Carolina could not be arrested and tried for a theft committed before the state seceded. In another opinion, issued with respect to the libel of a slave ship, he maintained that the law providing for prosecution of offenses against the United States was not authorized by the Constitution and, in fact, violated its ex post facto clause, unless the seceding state had expressly reserved the right of prosecution. The case pending in Florida was accordingly dismissed upon the motion of the Confederate district attorney.[42]

Of course, the main constitutional issues in the four-year history of the Confederacy were related to the conduct of the war and especially to the intrusion of national power on state sovereignty and personal liberty. In the South, as in the North, the war soon exposed a fundamental disagreement about priorities, well illustrated in the contrasting attitudes of Jefferson Davis and Alexander H. Stephens. Davis, a man firmly committed to southern independence, believed that military victory must be pursued even at the cost of some constitutional strain; Stephens, the reluctant secessionist with deep misgivings about the war, insisted that constitutional rights must be maintained, even at some risk to military efficiency. The tension between these two general points of view was present in various controversies over specific wartime issues, including confiscation of enemy property, taxation, currency, the writ of habeas corpus, conscription, and impressment of military supplies.

Seizure of enemy property was a belligerent's right under the law of nations, but Confederate officials, for propaganda reasons, preferred to justify the Sequestration Act of August 27, 1861, as a retaliatory response to the confiscation law recently passed by the United States Congress. The act of August 27 assigned exclusive jurisdiction in sequestration proceedings to the Confederate district courts. Its constitutionality was challenged and upheld in several states, including South Carolina, where Judge Andrew G. McGrath rejected the strict-constructionist arguments of counsel and declared that the power of confiscation stemmed from the power to make war.[43] The act also provided that the money realized from the sale of sequestered property should be used to compensate Confederate citizens who had suffered property losses at the hands of the United States government. A Board of Sequestration Commissioners was created to administer this part of the act by examining claims and awarding payments, subject to congressional approval. Congress, it should be added, never established the court of claims required by the Constitution. As a consequence, the many claims of Confederate citizens against their own government were handled by various department heads and governmental agencies without any overall coordination.[44]

During the first two years of the war, the Confederacy followed a policy of light taxation and heavy borrowing, with inflation as the inevitable consequence. By the spring of 1863, government leaders were well aware that painful new taxes must be imposed. Their unpopular task was made all the more difficult by constitutional limitations. The framers of the Confederate Constitution had included the requirement adopted in 1787 that direct taxes, like representation, be apportioned among the states according to population, with slaves counting as three-fifths of free persons. Thoughtlessly, the framers had also included the 1787 provision that the apportionment must be based upon an enumeration to be taken within three years of the meeting of the first Congress. Since the phrase "direct taxes" was interpreted as referring principally to taxes on land and slaves, it appeared that a census, utterly impracticable in wartime, would have to precede the levying of any tax upon the principal wealth of the Confederacy. In a sweeping revenue measure passed on April 24, 1863, Congress did its best to avoid the constitutional problem by taxing personal property, income, occupations, and agricultural production.[45] The constitutionality of the law was nevertheless frequently challenged, and Davis met the issue head-on in his message to

Congress on December 7, arguing in effect that the apportionment requirement should be ignored until its implementation became feasible.[46] Congress responded in February 1864 by levying a tax of five percent on all real and personal property.[47] Thus the exigencies of war at last overrode a troublesome provision of the Constitution.

Despite inflationary pressures, the Confederate Congress, unlike its counterpart in Washington, refused to enact a legal tender law requiring that treasury notes and other paper currency be accepted in payment of any debt, public or private. Opponents of the proposed legislation argued successfully that it was not only unwise but unauthorized by the Constitution. However, a number of state governments, ignoring even clearer constitutional restraints, did pass legal tender acts of one kind or another.[48] And Congress, in February 1864, enacted a funding law that may well have been unconstitutional, although it was apparently never tested in the courts.[49]

In this civil war, as in all such conflicts, both sides found it necessary to deal repressively with internal problems of disloyalty, resistance, and disorder. Both governments resorted to arbitrary arrests, suspended the writ of habeas corpus, and established martial law in sensitive areas. Not surprisingly, both thereby provoked angry protest and much public debate about civil rights in wartime. The Confederate Congress authorized suspension of the writ of habeas corpus in two separate periods totaling only seventeen months of the war. Although expressly sanctioned by the Constitution, suspension aroused much hostility, owing in considerable part to its close association with the stringencies of martial law and the enforcement of conscription.[50] The opposition was particularly strong in North Carolina and in Georgia, where Vice President Stephens openly encouraged resistance to what he considered the dictatorial tendencies of the Davis administration.[51]

Opponents in Congress were able to prevent renewal of the suspension law when it expired on February 11, 1863, and for a year Davis simply got along without the power as best he could. Then, in some desperation, he sent an urgent message to Congress explaining the difficulty of suppressing espionage, conspiracy, and other forms of disloyalty through ordinary civil process. "Must the independence for which we are contending . . . be put in peril," he asked, "for the sake of conformity to the technicalities of the law of treason?"[52] Congress responded with new legislation permitting suspension of the writ for a period of less than six months. In the ensuing public uproar, several state legislatures pronounced the law unconstitutional.[53] When it expired on August 1, 1864, there was no further renewal, despite additional appeals from Davis, whose last official words on the subject were these, written three weeks before the fall of Richmond: "On Congress must rest the responsibility of declining to exercise a power conferred by the Constitution as a means of public safety, to be used in periods of national peril resulting from foreign invasion. If our present circumstances are not such as were contemplated when this power was conferred, I confess myself at a loss to imagine any contingency in which this clause of the Constitution will not remain a dead letter."[54]

Suspension of the writ of habeas corpus remained a serious issue in the later stages of the war primarily because of its relation to conscription, which the Confederacy instituted in April 1862 and broadened in subsequent legislation.[55] The draft offended southern sensibilities and put added strain on southern unity. It was grimly defended as a military necessity and heavily attacked as an invasion of state sovereignty and personal liberty. Critics maintained that the power of the

Confederate government to "raise and support armies" extended only to enlisting volunteers and calling out the militia. Attorney General Watts rejected that argument in an official opinion presented to Davis in May 1862. He held that there was no constitutional limitation on the mode of raising armies, except that it must not violate any other clause of the Constitution.[56] Similar views prevailed in all the state supreme court decisions rendered on the subject.[57] Thus the constitutionality of conscription came to be fairly well established as a general principle, but with its operation in detail there was a great amount of hostile interference by state and local officials.

Among the leading antagonists were certain state governors, notably Zebulon B. Vance of North Carolina and Joseph E. Brown of Georgia. Vance supported conscription, but political pressures at home drove him into quarrels with the Davis administration over the manner of its enforcement. Brown challenged the constitutionality of the draft and impeded its operation in every way he could. He used his power of exemption to protect an absurdly large number of public officials from the draft, including, it was said, more than two thousand justices of the peace, many of whom never held a court, and about three thousand militia officers, most of whom had no men to command.[58] No less obstructive were the many lower-court judges who granted writs of habeas corpus for persons claiming exemption of one kind or another. General Robert E. Lee complained of the resulting "drain upon the strength of the Army" and pointed to a fellow Virginian as one flagrant example: "He has a contract to convey the mails on an unimportant route in Alabama. He resides in Richmond, where he is carrying on his business, and has never seen his route, as I am informed. Yet the court discharged him."[59] In North Carolina, the pattern of judicial resistance was set by the chief justice of the state supreme court, Richmond M. Pearson, who discharged more than a hundred conscripts during the first few months of 1864 alone.[60] Davis had Pearson especially in mind when he asked Congress to restore the power of suspension. Otherwise, he said, "in every case the enrollment will be followed by the writ, and every enrolling officer will be kept in continual motion to and from the judge, until the embarrassment and delay will amount to the practical repeal of the law."[61] In order to limit the obstructiveness of local judges, the Davis administration seems to have followed a policy of "honoring the decree of a civil court in a particular case but rejecting it as a general rule of action for the conscript officers."[62]

Conscription was bad enough in a society that prized individualism, but for many southerners the ultimate outrage was military impressment of food and other supplies, which resulted in much aggravation, hardship, and petty injustice. Although some commanders resorted to impressment early in the war, Congress did not give it statutory sanction until March 26, 1863.[63] The law of that date served a desperate need, but often it was used to justify irregular and heavy-handed behavior that degenerated at times into plain brigandage. In Georgia, the chronically restive Governor Brown secured passage of legislation making unauthorized impressment punishable with thirty-nine lashes and ten years in prison.[64] The principal constitutional issue was not impressment itself but the government's determined efforts to pay less than the progressively inflated market value for requisitioned products. Only in Georgia did the issue come before a state supreme court. There, the power of impressment in wartime was affirmed, but the law in question was held to be partly invalid because it did not make adequate provision for the "just compensation" required by the Constitution.[65]

In the many vigorous public debates over impressment and

conscription and other wartime practices, there is ample evidence that constitutionalism remained a vital force throughout the short life of the Confederacy. Of course constitutional argument often served as a mask for other purposes, but it also gave expression to a basic cultural outlook that significantly influenced southern judgment and southern behavior. A constitutional system, if working properly, is conducive to orderliness and stability in human affairs. At the same time, it lays salutary restraint upon the will of the majority. With good reason, then, the slaveholding South, a minority section much in need of social stability, was distinctively and emphatically constitution-minded.

States-rights constitutionalism, though first formulated by the Jeffersonians, did not become a peculiarly southern doctrine until the 1820s, and throughout the antebellum period, as we have seen, it continued to be only one of two strategies followed in the defense of slavery. The other was a strategy of majoritarian politics that maximized southern influence in national affairs. The logic of states-rights theory led to nullification and secession, but even after the Republican victory in 1860, southerners were divided on the question of whether slavery could be protected more effectively inside or outside the Federal Union. The advocates of separation carried the day, first in seven states and then in four more. Secession was a formal process that suited the southern taste for constitutional order, but the war that soon followed brought disorder, and, ironically, proved especially dangerous to the very things that southern independence was supposed to protect—namely, slavery, state sovereignty, and constitutional rights. No doubt the growing resistance to administration policies on constitutional grounds had some negative effect on the prosecution of the war. Historians, however, are no longer disposed to accept the thesis of Frank

L. Owsley that the Confederacy "died of state rights."[66] More important, perhaps, is the strong possibility that the disastrous decline of morale in the later stages of the war resulted in part from a widespread feeling among the southern people of having already lost much of what they were fighting for.

Notes

One. Southern State Constitutions

1. Gordon S. Wood, *The Creation of the American Republic, 1776–1787* (Chapel Hill: University of North Carolina Press, 1969), 128.
2. The first American constitutions (including the Articles of Confederation) were drafted by legislatures or by conventions that also engaged in legislation. Massachusetts in 1779–80 set the pattern of electing a body of delegates for the exclusive purpose of framing a constitution. That example was followed by New Hampshire in 1783–84 and by every state thereafter. See Willi Paul Adams, *The First American Constitutions: Republican Ideology and the Making of the State Constitutions in the Revolutionary Era*, trans. Rita and Robert Kimber (Chapel Hill: University of North Carolina Press, 1980), 86–93.
3. See Julius Goebel, Jr., *History of the Supreme Court of the United States*, Vol. 1, *Antecedents and Beginnings to 1801* (New York: Macmillan Co., 1971), 125–42; Charles Grove Haines, *The American Doctrine of Judicial Supremacy* (New York: Russell and Russell, 1959), 88–121.
4. This achievement of John Adams and the significance of the Massachusetts constitution of 1780 are generally ignored by textbooks in American history.
5. Fletcher M. Green, *Constitutional Development in the South Atlantic States, 1776–1860: A Study in the Evolution of Democracy*, (Chapel Hill: University of North Carolina Press, 1930).
6. Adams, *First American Constitutions*, 55–56.

164 Notes to Chapter One

7. See Donald S. Lutz, *Popular Consent and Popular Control: Whig Political Theory in the Early State Constitutions* (Baton Rouge: Louisiana State University Press, 1980), 63–68.
8. Green, *Constitutional Development*, 60–73; Walter Farleigh Dodd, *The Revision and Amendment of State Constitutions* (Baltimore: Johns Hopkins Press, 1910), 12–23; John Alexander Jameson, *A Treatise on Constitutional Conventions; Their History, Powers, and Modes of Proceeding* (Chicago: Callaghan and Co., 1887), 122–26, 128–30, 132–37; John A. Munroe, *History of Delaware*, 2d ed. (Newark: University of Delaware Press, 1984), 69–70.
9. Jameson, *Constitutional Conventions*, 135–36; Ethel K. Ware, *A Constitutional History of Georgia* (New York: Columbia University Press, 1947), 62–64.
10. Dodd, *Revision of State Constitutions*, 64–65. Exceptions were Delaware (1831), Mississippi (1832), and Arkansas (1836). In a number of books it is stated mistakenly that the Mississippi constitution of 1817 was submitted, but see Winbourne Magruder Drake, "The Framing of Mississippi's First Constitution," *Journal of Mississippi History* 29 (1967): 323n.
11. Isidor Loeb, "Constitutions and Constitutional Conventions in Missouri," *Missouri Historical Review* 16 (1922): 195–96; Munroe, *History of Delaware*, 120–23.
12. The seven new southern states were Louisiana (1812), Mississippi (1817), Alabama (1819), Missouri (1821), Arkansas (1836), Florida (1838), and Texas (1845). The nine revisory constitutions were adopted by Virginia (1830), Delaware (1831), Mississippi (1832), Tennessee (1835), Louisiana (1845), Kentucky (1850), Maryland (1851), Virginia (1851), and Louisiana (1852). For a tabular summary of the first century of American constitution-making, see Jameson, *Constitutional Conventions*, 643–55.
13. The ten new free states were Ohio (1803), Indiana (1816), Illinois (1818), Maine (1820), Michigan (1837), Iowa (1846), Wisconsin (1848), California (1850), Oregon (1857), and Minnesota (1858). The twelve constitutions for states already in the Union were adopted by Connecticut (1818), Massachusetts (1821), New York (1821), Pennsylvania (1838), Rhode Island (1842), New Jersey (1844), New York (1846), Illinois (1848), Michigan (1850), Indiana (1851), Ohio (1851), and Iowa (1857).
14. Francis Newton Thorpe, ed., *The Federal and State Constitutions, Colonial Charters, and other Organic Laws of the States, Territories, and*

Colonies Now or Heretofore Forming the United States of America, 7 vols. (Washington: Government Printing Office, 1909), 5:2798; Harold J. Counihan, "The North Carolina Constitutional Convention of 1835: A Study in Jacksonian Democracy," North Carolina Historical Review 46 (1969): 335–64; Green, Constitutional Development, 225–33.

15. Thorpe, Constitutions, 1:568, 2:785, 3:1701.
16. Jameson, Constitutional Conventions, 550–51. The two kinds of extraordinary legislative action most commonly required were passage by more than a simple majority and passage by two successive legislatures.
17. Thorpe, Constitutions, 2:802–9. The amendment establishing the supreme court was passed in 1835, but because of various delays, the court did not actually come into existence until 1845.
18. Herman V. Ames, The Proposed Amendments to the Constitution of the United States during the First Century of Its History, vol. 2 of Annual Report of the American Historical Association for the Year 1896 (Washington: Government Printing Office, 1897), 186–89, 195–97.
19. "Each generation is as independent as the one preceding, as that was of all which had gone before. It has then, like them, a right to choose for itself the form of government it believes most promotive of its own happiness; . . . and it is for the peace and good of mankind, that a solemn opportunity of doing this every nineteen or twenty years, should be provided by the constitution." Jefferson to Samuel Kercheval, July 12, 1816, in Thomas Jefferson, Writings: Autobiography; A Summary View of the Rights of British America; Notes on the State of Virginia; Public Papers; Addresses, Messages, and Replies; Miscellany; Letters (New York: Library of America, 1984), 1402.
20. Thorpe, Constitutions, 6:3267; Green, Constitutional Development, 201–2.
21. Dodd, Revision of State Constitutions, 46–49.
22. Kirk H. Porter, A History of Suffrage in the United States (Chicago: University of Chicago Press, 1918), 12; Adams, First American Constitutions, 295–307; Francis Newton Thorpe, A Constitutional History of the American People, 1776–1850, 2 vols. (New York: Harper and Brothers, 1898), 1:68–71, 77–79, 82–83, 93–96; Gregory Glen Schmidt, "Republican Visions: Constitutional Thought and Constitutional Revision in the Eastern United States, 1815–1830" (Ph.D. diss., University of Illinois at Urbana-Champaign, 1981), 329–30.

23. Thorpe, *Constitutions*, 6:3251, 3258–59. Under the 1778 constitution, voters in South Carolina were required only to believe in the existence of God and a future state of rewards and punishments. Officeholders, on the other hand, had to be Protestants. Ibid., 6:3252.
24. Ibid., 1:284, 566; 2:779; 3:1690, 1700; 4:2044, 2061; 5:2793, 2798–99; 6:3250, 3252. The declaration of rights in the Tennessee constitution of 1796 contained this provision: "No religious test shall ever be required as a qualification to any office or public trust under this State." Yet elsewhere the same constitution excluded from office any person who denied "the being of God or a future state of rewards, and punishments." This striking contradiction was not just an error of the moment; for it was retained in the constitution of 1834. Apparently, the exclusion of nonbelievers from office was not regarded in Tennessee as falling within the meaning of a "religious test." Ibid., 6:3420, 3422, 3427, 3437.
25. Ibid., 1:568; 2:786; 6:3259.
26. Thorpe, *Constitutions*, 3:1715; 5:2799; Green, *Constitutional Development*, 183–85. The Maryland constitution of 1776 required belief in the Christian religion. An amendment in 1825 permitted Jews to qualify by subscribing to a belief in a future state of rewards and punishments. These provisions were retained in the constitution of 1851.
27. Counihan, "North Carolina Convention," 351–53; Green, *Constitutional Development*, 183. The article, as amended, read: "No person who shall deny the being of God, or the truth of the Christian religion, or the divine authority of the Old or New Testament, or who shall hold religious principles incompatible with the freedom or safety of the State, shall be capable of holding any office or place of trust or profit in the civil department of this State."
28. Thorpe, *Constitutions*, 1:562, 570, 571; 2:779, 791, 792, 796; 3:1381–82, 1383, 1384–85, 1691, 1694; 4:2035–36, 2037, 2039; 5:2790, 2791; 6:3259–60, 3415, 3417.
29. Ibid., 7:3815–16, 3823–24, 3838.
30. Ibid., 1:584. The Missouri constitution required that members of the legislature be taxpayers. There was no such requirement for suffrage or for the governorship. Ibid., 4:2151.
31. Property qualifications for office were removed as follows: Maryland by amendment in 1810, Mississippi in its constitution of 1832, Tennessee in its constitution of 1834, Georgia by amendments in 1835 and

1847, and Louisiana in its constitution of 1845. Ibid., 2:805–6, 809; 3:1393, 1395, 1397, 1705; 4:2052, 2053, 2058; 6:3430, 3432.
32. Thorpe, *Constitutions*, 1:574; 2:789; 3:1705; 5:2790, 2799; 6:3267; 7:3832–33.
33. Tennessee's 1796 constitution did require a freehold *or* six months' residence in the county. What this amounted to was a residence requirement, waived for anyone who acquired a freehold. Thorpe, *Constitutions*, 6:3418; and see Stanley J. Folmsbee, Robert E. Corlew, and Enoch L. Mitchell, *Tennessee: A Short History* (Knoxville: University of Tennessee Press, 1969), 108–9.
34. Thorpe, *Constitutions*, 1:99, 271; 2:673; 3:1269, 1382, 1394; 4:2035, 2051, 2152; 6:3418, 3549. The Mississippi constitution of 1817 required taxpaying or militia service as a qualification for suffrage.
35. The three states still having property qualifications in 1840 were Rhode Island, Virginia, and North Carolina (for electors of the upper house); the eight states having taxpaying qualifications in 1840 were New Hampshire, Connecticut, Massachusetts, New Jersey, Pennsylvania, Delaware, Ohio, and Louisiana. In addition, North Carolina had a taxpaying qualification for electors of the lower house. The freehold requirement in the New Jersey constitution of 1776 had been changed to a taxpaying requirement by statutory interpretation in 1807. New Hampshire had a poll tax, and so its taxpaying requirement was equivalent to universal suffrage. See Chilton Williamson, *American Suffrage from Property to Democracy, 1760–1860* (Princeton, N.J.: Princeton University Press, 1960), 180–81. By 1860, all property qualifications had been abolished, but North Carolina, Delaware, and five northern states retained their taxpaying requirements.
36. Ralph A. Wooster, *The People in Power: Courthouse and Statehouse in the Lower South, 1850–1860* (Knoxville: University of Tennessee Press, 1969), 4–7, 108–9.
37. Jerome J. Nadelhaft, *The Disorders of War: The Revolution in South Carolina* (Orono: University of Maine at Orono Press, 1981), 208–9, maintains that the South Carolina constitution of 1790 made the backcountry "the most powerful section in both branches of the legislature," but he arrives at this conclusion by treating the Charleston district and the rest of the low country as two separate sections. Certainly the struggle over apportionment continued after 1790 in South Carolina. For the more traditional view that Nadelhaft challenges, see William A. Schaper, "Sectionalism and Representation in South

Carolina," American Historical Association *Annual Report,* 1900, vol. 1 (Washington: Government Printing Office, 1901), 407–37; John Harold Wolfe, *Jeffersonian Democracy in South Carolina* (Chapel Hill: University of North Carolina Press, 1940), 49–53.

38. The South Carolina constitution of 1778 apportioned representation in specific terms but made provision for reapportionment in 1785 and every fourteen years thereafter on a "taxable property" basis. Reapportionment did not take place in 1785 but was achieved in the constitution of 1790, again in specific terms, without a general formula for future reapportionment. Thorpe, *Constitutions,* 6:3250–51, 3258–59; Schaper, "Sectionalism and Representation," 368–69, 378–79.

39. See the chart in Robert G. Dixon, Jr., *Democratic Representation: Reapportionment in Law and Politics* (New York: Oxford University Press, 1968), 62–63.

40. Senate seats might be apportioned equally among the counties, as in Georgia and in North Carolina until 1835; or according to white population, as in Alabama, Arkansas, Missouri, and Texas; or according to white population plus three-fifths of slaves, as in Florida; or according to taxes paid, as in North Carolina after 1835. Thorpe, *Constitutions,* 1:100, 275; 2:676, 791–92; 4:2152; 5:2790, 2794–95; 6:3552.

41. Ibid., 1:100, 275–76; 3:1265, 1382; 4:2036, 2151–52; 6:3266, 3430, 3552. An amendment added to the South Carolina constitution in 1808 required that half the seats in the lower house be apportioned according to the number of white inhabitants and half according to taxes paid.

42. Ibid., 3:1393, 1395, 1412, 1721. The Louisiana constitution of 1845 based senate apportionment on total population, but the house was apportioned according to qualified electors. The constitution of 1852 used total population as the basis for apportionment of both chambers. Apportionment of the lower house according to total population was provided for in the Maryland constitution of 1851. It should be noted also that the Tennessee constitution of 1796 based apportionment on taxable inhabitants, which for a time may have been interpreted as including slaves. Compare Chase C. Mooney, "The Question of Slavery and the Free Negro in the Tennessee Constitutional Convention of 1834," *Journal of Southern History* 12 (1946): 506, with Folmsbee, Corlew, and Mitchell, *Tennessee,* 174.

43. Thorpe, *Constitutions,* 2:676, 791–92, 3:1708; 5:2794–95. The "federal number," adopted by North Carolina in 1835 and used by Maryland from 1837 to 1851, meant counting the free inhabitants and three-fifths of the slaves. Georgia, however, counted white inhabitants and

three-fifths of all blacks, thereby lumping free blacks with slaves. Florida counted white inhabitants and three-fifths of slaves, thereby omitting free blacks from the calculation. Mississippi and Alabama, at the time of their entry into the Union, considered and rejected the three-fifths formula. See Drake, "Mississippi's First Constitution," 314–15; Malcolm Cook McMillan, *Constitutional Development in Alabama, 1798–1901: A Study in Politics, the Negro, and Sectionalism* (Chapel Hill: University of North Carolina Press, 1955), 36.

44. *Proceedings and Debates of the Virginia State Convention of 1829–30* (Richmond: Samuel Shepherd and Co. for Ritchie and Cook, 1830), 70, 76.
45. Ibid., 417–18.
46. George Brown Oliver, "A Constitutional History of Virginia, 1776–1860" (Ph.D. diss., Duke University, 1959), 382–89, 420–30; Alison Goodyear Freehling, *Drift Toward Dissolution: The Virginia Slavery Debate of 1831–32* (Baton Rouge: Louisiana State University Press, 1982), 36–81; Dickson D. Bruce, Jr., *The Rhetoric of Conservatism: The Virginia Convention of 1829–30 and the Conservative Tradition in the South* (San Marino, Calif.: Huntington Library, 1982), 60–66.
47. Oliver, "Constitutional History of Virginia," 395–409. The constitution provided for reapportionment by the legislature in 1865, but if the two houses could not agree upon a principle of representation, the governor was to submit a choice of four plans to the voters. Thorpe, *Constitutions*, 7:3833–38.
48. *Proceedings and Debates*, 162.
49. Donald C. Butts, "The 'Irrepressible Conflict': Slave Taxation and North Carolina's Gubernatorial Election of 1860," *North Carolina Historical Review* 58 (1981): 44–66. For the partial adoption of ad valorem taxation of slaves in Tennessee (slaves under twelve and over fifty years of age were exempted), see Mooney, "Question of Slavery," 506–7.
50. Butts, "Irrepressible Conflict," 46.
51. Thorpe, *Constitutions*, 1:565–66; 2:778; 3:1687; 5:2787; 6:3243–44; 7:3815. Adams, *First American Constitutions*, 266–71. For example, the Virginia constitution declared: "The legislative, executive and judiciary departments shall be separate and distinct, so that neither exercises the powers properly belonging to the other: nor shall any person exercise the powers of more than one of them at the same time." The Maryland, North Carolina, and Georgia constitutions contained similar statements. The Delaware and South Carolina docu-

ments forbade holding executive and legislative offices at the same time.

52. Thorpe, *Constitutions*, 1:563; 2:781; 3:1695–96, 1699; 5:2791; 6:3243–44; 7:3816–17. The executive had the veto in the South Carolina constitution of 1776, but not in that of 1778 or 1790. In the first constitutions of Delaware and South Carolina, the executive was called "president."
53. Quoted in Charles C. Thach, Jr., *The Creation of the Presidency, 1775–1789: A Study in Constitutional History* (1923; reprint, Baltimore: Johns Hopkins Press, 1969), 29.
54. Thorpe, *Constitutions*, 2:778, 785; Green, *Constitutional Development*, 84; Ware, *Constitutional History of Georgia*, 35, 65.
55. Jefferson, *Writings*, 243–55; James Madison, "Vices of the Political System of the United States," *The Papers of James Madison*, vol. 9, ed. Robert A. Rutland, William M. E. Rachal, et al. (Chicago: University of Chicago Press, 1975), 345–58.
56. Thorpe, *Constitutions*, 1:103–4, 277, 278–79; 2:666, 668; 3:1267–68, 1384–86; 4:2039, 2040, 2156; 6:3417, 3556, 3558.
57. Ibid., 7:3827.
58. Georgia gave the governor the veto in 1789; Delaware and Maryland accorded him important appointive powers. Ibid., 1:573; 2:788; 3:1719.
59. Ibid., 1:107, 573, 575; 3:1281–84, 1385, 1387, 1697, 1699; 4:2040, 2042, 2159; 5:2791; 6:3263–64; 7:3827. Georgia did not yet have a supreme court. Judges of the state's inferior and superior courts were elected by the voters for relatively brief terms. Ibid., 2:798, 804; Albert Berry Saye, *A Constitutional History of Georgia, 1732–1968*, rev. ed. (Athens: University of Georgia Press, 1970), 177–86. The South Carolina constitution of 1790 lodged the judicial power in such courts as the legislature should choose to establish. Not until 1824 was the equivalent of a supreme court created with appellate jurisdiction in both law and equity. Thorpe, *Constitutions*, 6:3263; Donald Senese, "Building the Pyramid: The Growth and Development of the State Court System in Antebellum South Carolina, 1800–1860," *South Carolina Law Review* 24 (1972): 365. The Tennessee constitution of 1796 likewise left the judicial system to be designed by the legislature, which established a supreme court in 1809. The constitution of 1834 gave the court constitutional status. *History of Tennessee from the Earliest Time to the Present (1887), Including Its Early Explorations*

and *Pre-Historic Races, Also Its Aboriginal and Pioneer Annals* (Nashville: Goodspeed Publishing Co., 1887), 369–71, 374; Thorpe, *Constitutions*, 6:3419.

60. In 1830, eight of the twelve southern constitutions provided for removal of judges by address or concurrent resolution of the legislature. By the 1850s, fourteen out of fifteen did so. There were some variations. For instance, the Louisiana constitution required a three-fourths rather than a two-thirds vote of both houses, and the Virginia constitution of 1851 required only a majority vote of the whole membership of each house. Thorpe, *Constitutions*, 1:107, 274; 2:672, 804, 806; 3:1270, 1284, 1300, 1387, 1401, 1420, 1729; 4:2042, 2057, 2159–60; 5:2798; 6:3268, 3435, 3554; 7:3828, 3848. For efforts to remove judicial officers by impeachment and on address, see Goodspeed's *History of Tennessee*, 372–74; James W. Ely, Jr., "'That no office whatever be held during life or good behavior': Judicial Impeachments and the Struggle for Democracy in South Carolina," *Vanderbilt Law Review* 30 (1977): 167–209; McMillan, *Constitutional Development in Alabama*, 47–48; Arndt M. Stickles, *The Critical Court Struggle in Kentucky, 1819–1829* (Bloomington, Ind., 1929), 45–47; Stephen A. Smith, "Impeachment, Address, and the Removal of Judges in Arkansas: An Historical Perspective," *Arkansas Law Review* 32 (1978–79): 256–57.

61. Stickles, *Critical Court Struggle*, 43–106; Frank F. Mathias, "The Relief and Court Struggle: Half-Way House to Populism," *Register of the Kentucky Historical Society* 71 (1973): 154–76.

62. Senese, "Building the Pyramid," 367–69, 373. The 1859 legislation placed above the court of appeals a court of errors, consisting of all law judges, chancellors, and appeals judges sitting together.

63. Edwin Arthur Miles, *Jacksonian Democracy in Mississippi* (Chapel Hill: University of North Carolina Press, 1960), 36–40; Winbourne Magruder Drake, "The Mississippi Constitutional Convention of 1832," *Journal of Southern History* 23 (1957): 359–60, 363–64.

64. Thorpe, *Constitutions*, 4:2055.

65. The seven states were Kentucky, Louisiana, Maryland, Missouri, Tennessee, Texas, and Virginia. Ibid., 3:1300, 1418, 1727–28; 4:2171–72; 6:3444; 7:3847; Oliver C. Hartley, *A Digest of the Laws of Texas* (Philadelphia: Thomas Cowperthwaite and Co., 1850), 84; Kermit L. Hall, "The Judiciary on Trial: State Constitutional Reform and the Rise of an Elected Judiciary, 1846–1860," *Historian* 45 (1982–83): 337n. Texas

made its courts elective by an amendment in 1850 that is not included in the Thorpe collection. By the early 1850s, nine supreme courts in the free states were popularly elected.

66. They were the eight states with elective supreme courts, plus Alabama, Arkansas, and Georgia. See the table in Evan Haynes, *The Selection and Tenure of Judges* (n.p.: National Conference of Judicial Councils, 1944), 101–35.
67. Thorpe, *Constitutions*, 4:2055.
68. Ibid., 1:114, 281; 2:684, 806; 3:1300, 1400, 1727; 4:2055, 2171; 6:3435, 3554; 7:3847. In Georgia, the length of the term was left to the legislature's discretion. The Maryland constitution of 1851 established a ten-year term but provided that no judge should serve past the age of seventy.
69. Hall, "Judiciary on Trial," 348–51.
70. The Virginia constitution of 1851 plainly acknowledged the power when it spoke of cases involving "the constitutionality of a law." Margaret Virginia Nelson, *A Study of Judicial Review in Virginia, 1789–1928* (New York: Columbia University Press, 1947), 220n. The Georgia constitution of 1861 stated: "Legislative Acts in violation of the fundamental law are void; and the Judiciary shall so declare them." Ware, *Constitutional History of Georgia*, 123.
71. *Bayard v. Singleton*, 1 Martin 42 (N.C. 1787); Haines, *American Doctrine*, 112–20.
72. William E. Nelson, "Changing Conceptions of Judicial Review: The Evolution of Constitutional Theory in the States, 1790–1860," *University of Pennsylvania Law Review* 120 (1972): 1169–70.
73. *The Opinion of Judge [Theodorick] Bland on the Right of the Judiciary to Declare an Act of Assembly Unconstitutional and also on the Constitutionality of the Act Investing the County Courts with Equity Jurisdiction* (Baltimore: F. Lucas, Jr., 1816). See also *Goddin v. Crump*, 35 Virginia 120, 150, 154 (1837); *Gilkeson v. the Frederick Justices*, 54 Virginia 577 (1856); *Flint River Steamboat Co. v. Foster*, 5 Georgia 194, 204 (1848); *Barnes v. Barnes*, 53 North Carolina 366, 369 (1861).
74. For example, in *Grimball v. Ross*, T.U.P. Charlton 175, 177–78 (Ga., 1808), Judge Charlton said that the power of judicial review was to be exercised only where the act in question was "directly in the teeth of the constitutional provision"; in *Bristoe v. Evans*, 2 Tennessee 341 (1815), 345–46, Judge John Overton said that a court should make

every effort to reconcile the law with the constitution, pronouncing it void only if its unconstitutionality was "plain and obvious"; and in *Dorman v. State*, 34 Alabama 216, 235 (1859), Judge Richard W. Walker declared: "So long as the limitations of the constitution are not transcended, the wisdom, policy, and justice of laws must be left to the discretion of the legislature." See also *Flint River Steamboat Co. v. Foster*, 5 Georgia 194, 209 (1848); *Regents of the University of Maryland v. Williams*, 9 Gill and Johnson 365, 383 (Md., 1838); *Hamilton v. St. Louis County Court*, 15 Missouri 3, 23 (1851); *Eyre v. Jacob, Sheriff*, 55 Virginia 422, 438 (1858).

75. Nelson, *Judicial Review in Virginia*, 35, says that approximately thirty-five such decisions were rendered before the Civil War, but some of these involved the constitutionality of administrative actions rather than of statutes. For a good summary of antebellum judicial review in Virginia, see Oliver, "Constitutional History of Virginia," 327–55.

76. *Kamper v. Hawkins*, 1 Virginia Cases 20 (1793), struck down a 1792 law giving chancery jurisdiction to district courts. *Crenshaw and Crenshaw v. the State River Co.*, 27 Virginia 245 (1828), nullified an 1819 law requiring mill owners to build and superintend locks. Judge John W. Green, in a concurring opinion, stressed separation of powers and declared: "The questions, whether the rights of the owners of mills, or of the public, for the purposes of navigation, are preferred by Law . . . are emphatically Judicial in their nature" (p. 275).

77. Any exact figure would be arbitrary because certain cases are ambiguous and difficult to classify with respect to judicial review.

78. *Brewer v. Bowman*, 9 Georgia 37 (1850), and *Parham v. the Justices of Decatur County*, 9 Georgia 341 (1851); *Trustees of the University of North Carolina v. Foy and Bishop*, 5 North Carolina 58 (1805); *Griffin v. Mixon*, 38 Mississippi 424 (1860); *Bayard v. Singleton*, 1 Martin 42 (N.C. 1787); *Wally's Heirs v. Kennedy*, 10 Tennessee, 554 (1831); *Barnes v. Barnes*, 53 North Carolina 366 (1861); *Nunn v. State*, 1 Georgia 243 (1846); *Ham v. McClaws*, 1 Bay 93 (S.C., 1789); *Fisher's Negroes v. Dabbs*, 14 Tennessee 119 (1834); *Green v. Weller*, 32 Mississippi 650 (1856).

79. *Flint River Steamboat Co. v. Foster*, 5 Georgia 194 (1848); *Dorman v. State*, 34 Alabama 216 (1859); *Brinsfield v. Carter*, 2 Georgia 143 (1847); *Lyon v. State Bank*, 1 Stewart (in 1 Alabama), 442 (1828); *Goddin v. Crump*, 35 Virginia 120 (1837); *Alcorn v. Hamer*, 38 Mississippi 652 (1860).

80. For the cases in which civil rights issues were raised, see Nelson, *Judicial Review in Virginia*, 45–50; Oliver, "Constitutional History of Virginia," 342–50.
81. Thorpe, *Constitutions*, 3:1688; 7:3814.
82. *The Federalist Papers* (New York: New American Library, 1961), 513 (no. 84).
83. *Bayard v. Singleton*, 1 Martin 42 (N.C. 1787); *Ogden v. Witherspoon*, 3 North Carolina 404 (1802); *Trustees of the University of North Carolina v. Foy and Bishop*, 5 North Carolina 58 (1805); *Stidger v. Rogers*, 2 Kentucky 52 (1801); *Enderman v. Ashby*, 2 Kentucky 53 (1801); *McIlvain v. Holmes*, 2 Kentucky 317 (1804). Instead of "due process of law," most state constitutions used the phrase "according to the law of the land." Ex post facto laws and laws impairing the obligation of contracts were forbidden to states, of course, by the Federal Constitution, but by the time of the Civil War, most southern state constitutions contained the same prohibitions.
84. Nelson, "Changing Conceptions of Judicial Review," 1183–84. Of course it was becoming common practice in sectional argument for southerners to maintain that the primary purpose of a constitution was protection of minorities against the potential tyranny of the majority. See Jesse T. Carpenter, *The South as a Conscious Minority, 1789–1861: A Study in Political Thought* (New York: New York University Press, 1930), 127–29.
85. James E. Herget, "The Missing Power of Local Governments: A Divergence between Text and Practice in Our Early State Constitutions," *Virginia Law Review* 60 (1976): 1001–3.
86. Albert Ogden Porter, *County Government in Virginia: A Legislative History, 1607–1904* (New York: Columbia University Press, 1947), 11–12; Jefferson, *Writings*, 233; Saye, *Constitutional History of Georgia*, 483–86; *A Century of Population Growth: From the First Census of the United States to the Twelfth, 1790–1900* (Washington: Government Printing Office, 1909), 60; Ralph A. Wooster, *Politicians, Planters and Plain Folk: Courthouse and Statehouse in the Upper South, 1850–1860* (Knoxville: University of Tennessee Press, 1975), 97; Wooster, *People in Power*, 82. In Louisiana and Tidewater South Carolina, the districts were called "parishes" instead of "counties."
87. Jefferson to John Taylor, July 21, 1816, in Paul Leicester Ford, ed., *The Writings of Thomas Jefferson*, 10 vols. (New York: G. P. Putnam's Sons, 1892–99), 10:53. In South Carolina and to some extent in Maryland, the control of local government, instead of being centralized, was

distributed among several bodies. In Georgia, the governing authority was the inferior court. The county court system eventually moved westward to Kentucky, Tennessee, Missouri, Arkansas, and Texas. Mississippi had a county court system too, but only until 1832. In Mississippi thereafter, and in Florida, Alabama, and Louisiana, various names were used to designate the county governing body. See Wooster, *People in Power*, 83–84, 88.

88. Wooster, *People in Power*, 83–85; Wooster, *Politicians, Planters and Plain Folk*, 99–103; Charles S. Sydnor, *The Development of Southern Sectionalism, 1819–1848* (Baton Rouge: Louisiana State University Press, 1948), 33–43.
89. Thorpe, *Constitutions*, 1:282; 7:3815, 3818.
90. Ibid., 4:2042, 2056; *Digest of the Laws of Mississippi* (New York: Alexander S. Gould, 1839), 680; John Hebron Moore, "Local and State Governments of Antebellum Mississippi," *Journal of Mississippi History* 44 (1962): 105.
91. Thorpe, *Constitutions*, 3:1303–5, 1729–32, 1738; 7:3849–50.
92. Oliver H. Prince, *Digest of the Laws of Georgia* (Milledgeville, Ga.: Grantland and Orme, 1822), 118. Thorpe, *Constitutions*, 2:802–3.
93. Thorpe, *Constitutions*, 1:105, 107; 4:2041.
94. Wooster, *Politicians, Planters and Plain Folk*, 105–8; Wooster, *People in Power*, 90–92. According to Wooster, the Alabama constitution of 1819 "provided that the commissioners of revenue and roads, sheriffs, county clerks, justices of the peace, and constables be chosen by the people." In fact, the constitution made only clerks and sheriffs elective. Other offices were subsequently added to the elective list by statute—justices of the peace and constables, for instance, by a law passed on the last day of 1822. Harry Toulmin, *A Digest of the Laws of the State of Alabama* (Cahaba, Ala.: Ginn and Curtis, 1823), 520.
95. Thorpe, *Constitutions*, 1:109, 284; 2:673–74; 675; 3:1309, 1405, 1406, 1726; 4:2041–42; 6:3437, 3560, 3561.
96. Ibid., 1:109; 2:680, 805; 3:1405; 4:2173; 6:3439.
97. Ibid., 1:98; 3:1726.
98. Ibid., 6:3561; Frederic L. Paxson, "The Constitution of Texas, 1845," *Southwestern Historical Quarterly* 18 (1914–15): 396.
99. Thorpe, *Constitutions*, 3:1727.
100. Ibid., 6:3562.
101. Ibid., 2:678–79.
102. James Willard Hurst, *The Growth of American Law: The Law Makers* (Boston: Little, Brown and Company, 1950), 240.

176 Notes to Chapter One

103. Thorpe, *Constitutions*, 3:1407; 6:3564–65.
104. Robert C. Reinders, "New England Influences on the Formation of Public Schools in New Orleans," *Journal of Southern History* 30 (1964): 181–95; John R. Ficklen, "The Origin and Development of the Public-School System in Louisiana," in *Report of the Commissioner of Education for the Year 1894–95*, 2 vols. (Washington: Government Printing Office, 1896), 2:1300–1303.
105. *Congressional Globe*, 35th Cong., 2d sess., 718; Reinders, "New England Influences," 193–4n; Carl F. Kaestle, *Pillars of the Republic: Common Schools and American Society, 1780–1860* (New York: Hill and Wang, 1983), 192–217.
106. The five states were Delaware, North Carolina, South Carolina, Georgia, and Louisiana. Three of these, North Carolina, South Carolina, and Georgia, were still operating under their eighteenth century constitutions, which characteristically did not mention slavery. Delaware's constitution contained relatively little superlegislation of any kind, and slavery was not a matter of critical importance in the state. Louisiana, together with South Carolina and Georgia, had relatively little reason to feel internally threatened about the future of slavery.
107. Thorpe, *Constitutions*, 1:111, 283; 2:680; 3:1272, 1726; 4:2062, 2154; 6:3432, 3563; 7:3840. Maryland's constitution simply forbade "any law abolishing the relation of master or slave." Ibid., 3:1726.
108. Ibid., 1:112, 274, 283; 3:1272–73; 4:2062, 2154; 6:3563–64.
109. For a summary, see Ira Berlin, *Slaves Without Masters: The Free Negro in the Antebellum South* (New York: Vintage Books, 1976), 138–39.
110. For the repressive laws, see Clement Eaton, *The Freedom-of-Thought Struggle in the Old South*, rev. ed. (New York: Harper and Row, 1964), 118–43. For extralegal repression, see Russel B. Nye, *Fettered Freedom: Civil Liberties and the Slavery Controversy, 1830–1860* (East Lansing: Michigan State College Press, 1949), 139–55.
111. Joan Wells Coward, *Kentucky in the New Republic: The Process of Constitution Making* (Lexington: University Press of Kentucky, 1979), 36–45.
112. On the distinctiveness of South Carolina, where suffrage amounted to little more than the right to vote for an all-powerful legislature, see James M. Banner, Jr., "The Problem of South Carolina," in Stanley Elkins and Eric McKitrick, eds., *The Hofstadter Aegis: A Memorial* (New York: Alfred A. Knopf, 1974), 60–93.
113. Williamson, *American Suffrage*, 210.
114. John D. Barnhart, *Valley of Democracy: The Frontier versus the Plan-

tation in the Ohio Valley, 1775–1818 (Bloomington: Indiana University Press, 1953), 102–3, 118–19; Peter H. Howard, *Political Tendencies in Louisiana*, rev. ed. (Baton Rouge: Louisiana State University Press, 1971), 20.

115. See, for example, the account of the struggle for constitutional reform in antebellum North Carolina in Green, *Constitutional Development*, 265–72, and in Thomas E. Jeffrey, "Beyond 'Free Suffrage': North Carolina Parties and the Convention Movement of the 1850s," *North Carolina Historical Review* 62 (1985): 387–419.
116. See, for example, Michael F. Holt, *The Political Crisis of the 1850s* (New York: John Wiley and Sons, 1978), 106–10.
117. George Phillip Parkinson, Jr., "Antebellum State Constitution-Making: Retention, Circumvention, Revision" (Ph.D. diss., University of Wisconsin, 1972), 37–39, 81–91.
118. Quoted in Jameson, *Constitutional Conventions*, 304.

Two. The South and the Federal Constitution

1. *The Federalist Papers* (New York: New American Library, 1961), 242–46 (no. 39).
2. Max Farrand, ed., *The Records of the Federal Convention of 1787*, 4 vols. (New Haven, Conn.: Yale University Press, 1911), 2:321, 325, 615–16.
3. Harold C. Syrett et al., eds., *The Papers of Alexander Hamilton*, 26 vols. (New York: Columbia University Press, 1961–79), 8:97–134.
4. In *The Federalist*, 286 (no. 44), Madison argued that popular control would be a greater restraint on Congress than on the state legislatures.
5. Ibid., 468–69 (no. 78).
6. General Henry Knox to Rufus King, July 15, 1787, quoted in Charles Warren, *The Making of the Constitution* (Boston, Little, Brown and Co., 1928), 308.
7. Farrand, *Records*, 1:21.
8. Ibid., 1:54; 2:27–28, 390–91; and see Charles F. Hobson, "The Negative on State Laws: James Madison, the Constitution, and the Crisis of Republican Government," *William and Mary Quarterly*, 3d ser., 36 (1979): 215–35.
9. Farrand, *Records*, 1:164–68, 250; 2:27–28, 390; Hobson, "Negative on State Laws," 227.
10. Section 25 of the Judiciary Act of 1789 gave the U.S. Supreme Court appellate jurisdiction in any case where the highest court of a state: 1)

declared a federal law or treaty to be unconstitutional; 2) upheld a state law challenged as contrary to the U.S. Constitution; or 3) ruled against a title, right, privilege, or exemption claimed under the Constitution or federal law. 1 *U.S. Statutes at Large* 85–86.

11. Herman V. Ames, ed., *State Documents on Federal Relations: The States and The United States* (New York: Da Capo Press, 1970), 4.
12. Merrill D. Peterson, *Thomas Jefferson and the New Nation: A Biography* (New York: Oxford University Press, 1970), 412–13; Jacob E. Cooke, "The Compromise of 1790," *William and Mary Quarterly*, 3d ser., 27 (1970): 523–45; Kenneth R. Bowling, "Dinner at Jefferson's: A Note on Jacob E. Cooke's 'The Compromise of 1790,'" *William and Mary Quarterly*, 3d ser., 28 (1971): 629–40, with a "Rebuttal" by Cooke, 640–48.
13. Ames, ed., *State Documents*, 9–10. Doyle Mathis, "Chisholm v. Georgia: Background and Settlement," *Journal of American History* 54 (1967–68): 19–29.
14. John C. Miller, *The Federalist Era, 1789–1801* (New York: Harper and Row, 1960), 46.
15. *Annals of Congress*, 1st Cong., 3d sess., col. 1960.
16. Miller, *Federalist Era*, 56–59; Peterson, *Jefferson*, 432–34.
17. John C. Miller, *Alexander Hamilton: Portrait in Paradox* (New York: Harper and Brothers, 1959), 264.
18. James Morton Smith, *Freedom's Fetters: The Alien and Sedition Laws and American Civil Liberties* (Ithaca, N.Y.: Cornell University Press, 1956), 94–155.
19. Henry Steele Commager, ed., *Documents of American History*, 7th ed., 2 vols. (New York: Appleton-Century-Crofts, 1963), 1:178–84; Dumas Malone, *Jefferson and His Time*, 6 vols. (Boston: Little Brown, 1948–81), 3:399–409; Adrienne Koch and Harry Ammon, "The Virginia and Kentucky Resolutions: An Episode in Jefferson's and Madison's Defense of Civil Liberties," *William and Mary Quarterly*, 3d ser., 5 (1948): 145–76.
20. Ames, ed., *State Documents*, 15–26.
21. Thomas Jefferson, *Writings: Autobiography; A Summary View of the Rights of British America; Notes on the State of Virginia; Public Papers; Addresses, Messages, and Replies; Miscellany; Letters* (New York: Library of America, 1984), 1138–41; Malone, *Jefferson*, 4:311–20.
22. *Annals of Congress*, 8th Cong., 1st sess., cols. 49–53, 61–62, 68–71.
23. Peterson, *Jefferson*, 689.
24. James M. Banner, Jr., *To the Hartford Convention: The Federalists and*

the *Origins of Party Politics in Massachusetts, 1789–1815* (New York: Alfred A. Knopf, 1970), 329–46.
25. Richmond *Enquirer*, Nov. 1, 1814, quoted in Thomas P. Abernethy, *The South in the New Nation, 1789–1819* (Baton Rouge: Louisiana State University Press, 1961), 422.
26. Ames, ed., *State Documents*, 45–50; Kenneth W. Treacy, "The Olmstead Case, 1778–1809," *Western Political Quarterly* 10 (1957): 675–91.
27. *Hunter v. Martin*, 18 Virginia 1, 58–59 (1815); Boyd Clifton Rist, "The Jeffersonian Crisis Revived: Virginia, the Court, and the Appellate Jurisdiction Controversy" (Ph.D. diss., University of Virginia, 1985), 195–200. The decision was reversed by the United States Supreme Court in *Martin v. Hunter's Lessee*, 1 Wheaton 304 (1816).
28. Ames, ed., *State Documents*, 89–91.
29. Jesse T. Carpenter, *The South as a Conscious Minority, 1789–1861: A Study in Political Thought* (New York: New York University Press, 1930), 3–4, 21–23.
30. James D. Richardson, ed., *A Compilation of the Messages and Papers of the Presidents*, 11 vols. (Washington: Bureau of National Literature, 1913), 1:550–53, 561, 569–70.
31. Norman K. Risjord, *The Old Republicans: Southern Conservatism in the Age of Jefferson* (New York: Columbia University Press, 1965), 177–82, 223–26. For an extensive treatment, see Rist, "Jeffersonian Crisis Revived," 137–387.
32. Robert L. Meriwether, W. Edwin Hemphill, and Clyde N. Wilson, eds., *The Papers of John C. Calhoun*, 17 vols. to date (New York: Columbia University Press, 1959–86), 1:403; Charles M. Wiltse, *John C. Calhoun, Nationalist, 1782–1828* (Indianapolis: Bobbs Merrill Co., 1944), 132–35.
33. *Reminiscences of James A. Hamilton, or Men and Events at Home and Abroad* (New York: Charles Scribner, 1869), 62.
34. Meriwether, Hemphill, and Wilson, eds., *Papers of Calhoun*, 10:301.
35. Wiltse, *Calhoun, Nationalist*, 390–98; William W. Freehling, *Prelude to Civil War: The Nullification Controversy in South Carolina, 1816–1836* (New York: Harper and Row, 1965), 158–65. Calhoun did not become a public advocate of nullification until 1831. See Charles M. Wiltse, *John C. Calhoun, Nullifier, 1829–1839* (Indianapolis: Bobbs Merrill Co., 1949), 113–15.
36. Glover Moore, *The Missouri Controversy, 1819–1821* (Lexington: University of Kentucky Press, 1953), 35; Don E. Fehrenbacher, *The South*

and *Three Sectional Crises* (Baton Rouge: Louisiana State University Press, 1980), 14–15.
37. Moore, *Missouri Controversy*, 53n, 55n.
38. Freehling, *Prelude to Civil War*, 60.
39. On the relation between slavery and the Nullification crisis, see ibid., 49–52, 255–59; Richard E. Ellis, *The Union at Risk: Jacksonian Democracy, States' Rights, and the Nullification Crisis* (New York: Oxford University Press, 1987), pp. 190–94.
40. Meriwether, Hemphill, and Wilson, eds., *Papers of Calhoun*, 10:494–532; August O. Spain, *The Political Theory of John C. Calhoun* (New York: Bookman Associates, 1951), 172–78, 186–207.
41. See Ellis, *Union at Risk*, 178–83, for a summing up of the book's thesis that Jackson's strategy during the Nullification crisis weakened his presidency and strengthened the hands of the nullifiers.
42. Ames, ed., *State Documents*, 178–85; Freehling, *Prelude to Civil War*, 265.
43. Ulrich Bonnell Phillips, "Georgia and State Rights," in *Annual Report of the American Historical Association for the Year 1901*, vol. 2 (Washington: Government Printing Office, 1902), 66–86.
44. In the broadest sense, to be sure, nullification and the concurrent majority both fitted into the Calhoun scheme of an institutionalized "mutual negative" as the basis for negotiated political consensus. See Walter Hartwell Bennett, *American Theories of Federalism* (University: University of Alabama Press, 1964), 128–51.
45. Richard K. Crallé, ed., *The Works of John C. Calhoun*, 6 vols. (New York: D. Appleton, 1888), 1:24–52; Spain, *Political Theory of Calhoun*, 129–55.
46. Farrand, *Records*, 1:486–87.
47. Ibid., 2:100.
48. Crallé, ed., *Works of Calhoun*, 1:392–95; Carpenter, *South as a Conscious Minority*, 96.
49. Carpenter, *South as a Conscious Minority*, 111.
50. Robert Manson Myers, ed., *The Children of Pride: A True Story of Georgia and the Civil War* (New Haven, Conn.: Yale University Press, 1972), 648.
51. William B. Trescot to William Porcher Miles, December 19, 1856, William Porcher Miles Papers, Southern Historical Collection, University of North Carolina.
52. Carpenter, *South as a Conscious Minority*, 180–81; Richard Malcolm Johnston and William Hand Browne, *Life of Alexander H. Stephens*, rev. ed. (Philadelphia: J. B. Lippincott, 1883), 375.

53. On the development of southern unity in defense of slavery, see William J. Cooper, Jr., *The South and the Politics of Slavery, 1828–1856* (Baton Rouge: Louisiana State University Press, 1978), 58–64.
54. Charles M. Wiltse, *John C. Calhoun, Sectionalist, 1840–1850* (Indianapolis: Bobbs Merrill Co., 1951), 161. Thomas Hart Benton, who hated Calhoun, stalked out before the vote.
55. Rhett to William Porcher Miles, Sept. 15, 1858, Miles Papers.
56. Roy Franklin Nichols, *The Disruption of American Democracy* (New York: MacMillan Co., 1948), 378, 384, 387–88, 391, 422, 427–28; Philip Shriver Klein, *President James Buchanan: A Biography* (University Park: Pennsylvania State University Press, 1962), 353–54, 368–69, 375, 378–79.
57. *Congressional Globe*, 35th Cong., 1st sess., 962.
58. *Prigg v. Pennsylvania*, 16 Peters 539, 611 (1842).
59. *Dred Scott v. Sandford*, 19 Howard 393, 451–52 (1857).

Three. The Confederacy as a Constitutional System

1. *The Richmond Examiner During the War; or, The Writings of John M. Daniel, with a Memoir of His Life, by His Brother, Frederick S. Daniel* (New York: 1868), 65–68.
2. Ibid., 19–20, 209, 214.
3. Kenneth M. Stampp, *The Imperiled Union: Essays on the Background of the Civil War* (New York: Oxford University Press, 1980), 257.
4. Richard E. Beringer, Herman Hattaway, Archer Jones, William N. Still, Jr., *Why the South Lost the Civil War* (Athens: University of Georgia Press, 1986), 66, 77. For an argument that "a spirit of Confederate nationalism failed to develop," because of the character of the southern social order, see Paul D. Escott, "The Failure of Confederate Nationalism: The Old South's Class System in the Crucible of War," in Harry P. Owens and James J. Cooke, eds., *The Old South in the Crucible of War* (Jackson: University Press of Mississippi, 1983), 15–28.
5. Emory M. Thomas, *The Confederate Nation, 1861–1865* (New York: Harper and Row, 1979), 28, 297–99; Emory M. Thomas, "Reckoning with Rebels," in Owens and Cooke, eds., *The Old South*, 12.
6. David M. Potter, *The Impending Crisis, 1848–1861*, completed and edited by Don E. Fehrenbacher (New York: Harper and Row, 1976), 469.
7. Steven A. Channing, "Slavery and Confederate Nationalism," in Wal-

ter J. Fraser, Jr., and Winfred B. Moore, Jr., eds., *From the Old South to the New: Essays on the Transitional South* (Westport, Conn.: Greenwood Press, 1981), 223.

8. Ulrich Bonnell Phillips, *The Life of Robert Toombs* (New York: Macmillan, 1913), 232. Joseph Hodgson, an Alabamian, in his book *The Cradle of the Confederacy: or, The Times of Troup, Quitman and Yancey* . . . (Mobile, 1876), 469, declared with some exaggeration: "That secession might be, and doubtless would be, a peaceable measure, was almost universally believed by the secession party of the South."

9. *Congressional Globe*, 36th Cong., 2d sess., p. 40.

10. Pierce to Davis, January 6, 1860, in Horace Greeley, *The American Conflict: A History of the Great Rebellion in the United States of America* . . . 2 vols. (Hartford, Conn.: O. D. Case, 1866–67), 1:512–13; Richmond *Enquirer*, Jan. 1, 3, March 8, May 8, 1861.

11. William R. Leslie, "The Confederate Constitution," *Michigan Quarterly Review* 2 (1963): 153.

12. Charles Robert Lee, Jr., *The Confederate Constitutions* (Chapel Hill: University of North Carolina Press, 1963), 60–122.

13. James H. Hammond to R. F. Simpson, November 22, 1860, in Carol Bleser, ed., *The Hammonds of Redcliffe* (New York: Oxford University Press, 1981), 90.

14. James D. Richardson, ed., *A Compilation of the Messages and Papers of the Confederacy, Including the Diplomatic Correspondence, 1861–1865*, 2 vols. (Nashville: United States Publishing Company, 1905), 1:36.

15. The United States Constitution and the Confederate Constitution are printed in parallel columns in Lee, *Confederate Constitutions*, 171–200.

16. Several efforts to provide for secession were rejected by the framers. The delegates, for example, voted six to one against a motion to include the declaration: "That the right of secession of any State from this Confederacy is expressly admitted, to be exercised by any State according to its pleasure." Only the South Carolina delegation supported it. *Journal of the Congress of the Confederate States of America, 1861–1865*, 7 vols. (Washington: Government Printing Office, 1904–5), 1:873, 877. One reason for the opposition, to be sure, was that any constitutional confirmation of a right of secession would have undercut the southern argument that the right was inherent in the sovereignty of each state. See Leslie, "Confederate Constitution," 156–58.

17. See William M. Robinson, Jr., "A New Deal in Constitutions," *Journal of Southern History* 4 (1938): 449–61, which concludes with the extravagant assertion that "the Constitution of the Confederate States, when viewed as a development in representative government, must be regarded as the peak contribution of America to political science."
18. Herman V. Ames, *The Proposed Amendments to the Constitution of the United States during the First Century of Its History*, vol. 2 of *Annual Report of the American Historical Association for the Year 1896* (Washington: Government Printing Office, 1897), 123–24.
19. The most tarnished public figure was Secretary of War John B. Floyd, a Virginian, who was eventually forced to resign. See Philip Shriver Klein, *President James Buchanan: A Biography* (University Park: Pennsylvania State University Press, 1962), 338–39, 377–80.
20. Donald Nieman, "Republicanism, the Confederate Constitution and the American Constitutional Tradition" (Paper presented at a conference on "The South and the American Constitutional Tradition," University of Florida, March 6–7, 1987).
21. Lee, *Confederate Constitutions*, 125–37.
22. Ibid., 138–39.
23. Ibid., 139–40.
24. Southern euphoria at the beginning of 1862 is illustrated in a Mobile *Register and Advertiser* editorial of February 6 declaring that in any negotiated peace, the North must give up the District of Columbia, Maryland, Kentucky, and Missouri. It was on that same day that Grant captured Fort Henry.
25. Richardson, ed., *Messages and Papers of the Confederacy*, 1:184–85, 188.
26. William M. Robinson, Jr., *Justice in Grey: A History of the Judicial System of the Confederate States of America* (Cambridge, Mass.: Harvard University Press, 1941), 420–21.
27. Richardson, ed., *Messages and Papers of the Confederacy*, 1:192.
28. Robinson, *Justice in Grey*, 423–24.
29. Quoted in ibid., 424.
30. *Journal of Congress*, 3:20, 32, 36, 38, 42, 44–45, 46, 47–48, 53, 56, 64, 66, 102, 106, 146, 164, 172, 174, 176–77; 6:537; 7:26, 281, 310, 758; Robinson, *Justice in Grey*, 426–29, 432–33, 470–73; John Witherspoon Dubose, *The Life and Times of William Lowndes Yancey*, 2 vols. (New York: Peter Smith, 1942), 739–40. Disagreement on the question of appellate jurisdiction over state court decisions, which probably prevented creation of a Confederate Supreme Court in 1863, had also been present in

the Constitutional Convention at Montgomery. A motion to prohibit such jurisdiction failed by a vote of three to three, with the seventh delegation evenly divided. *Journal of Congress*, 1:881.
31. Robinson, *Justice in Grey*, 434–35.
32. Ibid., 453–55. Benjamin, first attorney general, then secretary of war, and finally secretary of state in Davis's cabinet, was the President's most trusted associate, but he had made himself very unpopular in Congress and among the public at large. Campbell, former member of the United States Supreme Court, had lost favor in the South as a result of his informal negotiations with the Lincoln administration during the secession crisis. The possibility of Campbell's becoming Chief Justice was especially repugnant to his fellow Alabamian, Senator William Lowndes Yancey.
33. Richardson, ed., *Messages and Papers of the Confederacy*, 1:59, 100–01, 130–31, 156–66, 215–17, 262–68, 320–24, 408–12, 457–77, 553–63.
34. Ibid., 1:411.
35. Robinson, *Justice in Grey*, 28–29n.
36. Ibid., 33, 36–38.
37. See the exchange between Davis and Secretary of War George W. Randolph in *The War of the Rebellion: A Compilation of the Official Records of the Union and Confederate Armies*, 128 vols. (Washington: Government Printing Office, 1880–1901), ser. 4, 2:33–34, 41–42.
38. Robinson, *Justice in Grey*, 23.
39. Rembert W. Patrick, ed., *The Opinions of the Confederate Attorneys General, 1861–1865* (Buffalo, N.Y.: Dennis and Co., 1950), 264–65.
40. Albert Burton Moore, *Conscription and Conflict in the Confederacy* (New York: Macmillan Co., 1924), 163.
41. Robinson, *Justice in Grey*, 624.
42. Watts to John A. Reagan, December 27, 1862, and to Christopher G. Memminger, September 28, 1863, in Patrick, ed., *Opinions*, 197–203, 339–43.
43. John Christopher Schwab, *The Confederate States of America, 1861–1865: A Financial and Industrial History of the South during the Civil War* (New York: Charles Scribner's Sons, 1901), 116–18.
44. Robinson, *Justice in Grey*, 492–509.
45. Schwab, *Confederate States*, 291–93. Wilfred Buck Yearns, *The Confederate Congress* (Athens: University of Georgia Press), 199–200.
46. Richardson, *Messages and Papers of the Confederacy*, 1:363–67.
47. Schwab, *Confederate States*, 299–300; Yearns, *Confederate Congress*, 204–5.

48. Schwab, *Confederate States*, 98-100.
49. Ibid., 98; E. Merton Coulter, *The Confederate States of America, 1861-1865* (Baton Rouge: Louisiana State University Press, 1950), 160-61. The funding act, aimed at devaluing the currency in circulation, seemed to be in violation of the constitutional provision (Art. 1, Sec. 8, par. 4) that "no law of Congress shall discharge any debt contracted before the passage of the same."
50. Frank Lawrence Owsley, *State Rights in the Confederacy* (Chicago: University of Chicago Press, 1925), 150-62; Thomas B. Alexander and Richard E. Beringer, *The Anatomy of the Confederate Congress: A Study of the Influences of Member Characteristics on Legislative Voting Behavior, 1861-1865* (Nashville: Vanderbilt University Press, 1972), 166-73; Yearns, *Confederate Congress*, 150-55; Thomas, *Confederate Nation*, 150-52; Robinson, *Justice in Grey*, 383-405.
51. Owsley, *State Rights*, 162-76; May Spencer Ringold, *The Role of the State Legislatures in the Confederacy* (Athens: University of Georgia Press, 1966), 28-29. In Congress, according to Alexander and Beringer, *Anatomy of Confederate Congress*, 180-87, those who had been secessionists in 1860-1861 were strong supporters of suspension, and those who had been unionists were strongly opposed.
52. Richardson, ed., *Messages and Papers of the Confederacy*, 1:395-400; Robinson, *Justice in Grey*, 405-7.
53. Owsley, *State Rights*, 176-91. In a resolution passed March 19, 1864, for example, the Georgia legislature denounced the suspension act as "a dangerous assault upon the constitutional power of the courts and upon the liberty of the people." *Official Records*, ser. 4, 3:234-35.
54. Richardson, ed., *Messages and Papers of the Confederacy*, 1:548-49.
55. Moore, *Conscription and Conflict*, 13-16, 140-41, 308-9; Alexander and Beringer, *Anatomy of Confederate Congress*, 106-13.
56. Patrick, ed., *Opinions*, 95.
57. Moore, *Conscription and Conflict*, 168-70; J. G. de Roulhac Hamilton, "The State Courts and the Confederate Constitution," *Journal of Southern History* 4 (1938): 434-37; Sidney D. Brummer, "The Judicial Interpretation of the Confederate Constitution," in *Studies in Southern History and Politics Inscribed to William Archibald Dunning* (New York: Columbia University Press, 1914), 109-12.
58. *Official Records*, ser. 4, 3:345-49; Moore, *Conscription and Conflict*, 255-96; Richard E. Yates, "Zebulon B. Vance as a War Governor of North Carolina, 1862-1865," *Journal of Southern History* 3 (1937): 50-63; Paul D. Escott, "Georgia," in W. Buck Yearns, ed., *The Confederate*

Governors (Athens: University of Georgia Press, 1985), 69–82.
59. *Official Records*, ser. 4, 3:660–61.
60. Ibid., 3:200–201, 213, 238, 256; J. G. de Roulhac Hamilton, "The North Carolina Courts and the Confederacy," *North Carolina Historical Review* 4 (1927): 366–403.
61. Richardson, ed., *Messages and Papers of the Confederacy*, 1:399.
62. Moore, *Conscription and Conflict*, 182.
63. Yearns, *Confederate Congress*, 116–19; Owsley, *State Rights*, 219–24.
64. Owsley, *State Rights*, 226–71; Schwab, *Confederate States*, 202–7; *Official Records*, ser. 4, 2:943.
65. *Cunningham v. Campbell, et al.*, 33 Georgia 625; Brummer, "Judicial Interpretation," 126–28.
66. Owsley, *State Rights*, 1. Owsley saw a direct causal connection, for instance, between southern defeat and the refusal to continue suspension of the writ of habeas corpus (p. 202). For depreciation of the Owsley thesis, see David D. Scarboro, "North Carolina and the Confederacy: The Weakness of States' Rights during the Civil War," *North Carolina Historical Review* 56 (1979): 133–49; Curtis Arthur Amlund, *Federalism in the Confederacy* (Washington: Public Affairs Press, 1966), 113–14; Beringer, et al., *Why the South Lost*, 203–35.

Index

Abolitionism. *See* Antislavery movement
Adams, John, 11, 128, 163
Adams, John Quincy, 128, 134–35
African Colonization Society, xiii
Alabama: secession of, 5; and Compromise of 1850, 42; disunionism in, 44; as secessionist leader in 1858, pp. 53–54; limits judicial tenure, 98; local government in, 104, 175; abolishes imprisonment for debt, 105; divorce law in, 105; and nullification, 131; representation in, 168, 169; judicial system of, 172
Alden, John R., 9
Alien and Sedition Acts, 11, 120–21
American (Know-Nothing) party, 56, 58
American Revolution, 113, 139–40
Antislavery movement: southern responses to, xiii–xiv, xv, 30–31, 107–108; and manifest destiny, 34
Arkansas: secession of, 5; religious test in constitution, 88; limits judicial tenure, 98; constitution establishes county courts, 104; ratifies Confederate Constitution, 147; representation in, 168; judicial system of, 172; local government in, 175
Arkansas Territory, 16, 17, 18
Articles of Confederation, 10
Assumption of state debts, 118–19
Attorney general, Confederate, 152–54

Baldwin, Henry, 20
Banking, state, 105–106
Bank of the United States, 114–15, 119–20, 124, 151
Barney, William L., 49–50
Battle of New Orleans, xiii
Bayard v. Singleton, 99
Benjamin, Judah P., 52, 150–51, 152, 184
Benton, Thomas Hart, 41
Bestor, Arthur, xvi, 36
Beveridge, Albert J., 30
Bills of rights, state, 101–102
Black, Jeremiah S., 45–46
Border South: defined, 6; and Missouri Compromise, 19; abolition in, 30; and Compromise of 1850, pp. 41–42; and Lecompton struggle, 76
Breckinridge, John, 122
Brown, Albert Gallatin, 26

Brown, John, 6, 52, 62
Brown, Joseph E., 55, 158, 159
Buchanan, James, 45, 48, 54, 56, 57–58, 145

Calhoun, John C.: theory of Union, xviii–xix, 36–37, 130–32; as nationalist, 22; demands sectional equality, 26–27; and concurrent majority, 29, 132, 180; in crisis of 1850, p. 40; moves from nationalism to states rights, 126–28; compared to Jefferson, 127–28; and nullification, 130, 132, 179, 180; appointed secretary of state, 134; antiparty attitude of, 146
California: admission of, xiv, 36, 41, 42, 68–69; statehood movement in, 39–40; as Democratic state, 50; and election of 1856, p. 58
Campbell, John A., 150–51, 184
Carpenter, Jesse T., 9, 125
Cass, Lewis, 38–39
Channing, Steven A., 140
Charleston convention, 59, 61–62
Charleston *Mercury*, 61, 64
Charlton, T.U.P., 172
Chisholm v. Georgia, 118–19
Civil War: historiographical effect of, ix, 118; causes of, ix, x, xi, xvi, 1–7; battlefields of, xv; resolves issues of slavery and secession, xvi; as defense of right to secede, 138; and southern nationalism, 138–40; effect of, on Confederacy, 147; Confederacy begins to lose, 148; constitutional issues presented by, 154–60; destructive of Confederate purposes, 160–61

Clay, Clement C., 150
Clay, Henry, 40
Clayton, John M., 38
Clingman, Thomas L., 40
Clinton, DeWitt, 14, 72
Cobb, Howell, 44, 46
Cobb, Thomas W., 21
Cohens v. Virginia, 126
Common property doctrine, 36–37
Compromise of 1850, xiv, 40–44, 45, 51, 68–69
Concurrent majority, xix, 29, 132–33, 180
Confederacy (Confederate States of America): created by lower South, xv; purposes expressed in Confederate Constitution, xix–xx; and Fort Sumter, 65; moral isolation of, 137; geographic extent of, 147; legal continuity with U.S., 152–54; war policies of, 154–60; constitutionalism in, 160–61
Confederate nationalism. *See* Southern nationalism
Confederate South: and principle of entering wedge, xiv; defined, 6; and Compromise of 1850, p. 42; embraces principle of secessionism, 44
Confiscation of enemy property, 154–55
Congress, Continental, 83
Congress, Confederate: provisional, 148; fails to establish supreme court, 149–51; organizes executive branch, 151–52; and taxation, 155–56; refuses to enact legal tender law, 156; and habeas corpus

Index   189

suspension, 156–57, 185; authorizes impressment, 159
Congress, U.S.: sectional debates in, xi–xii, xiii; and crisis of 1846–50, xiii–xiv, 34–42; and final crisis of the Union, xvi, 62; early slavery issues in, 10, 12–13; and Missouri controversy, 14–23, 128–29; early policy of, on slavery in territories, 28; sectional strengths in, 29; southern power in, 46; passes Kansas-Nebraska Act, 51–52; and Lecompton Constitution, 53–55; sectional crises in, 55–56, 57; and final crisis, 62; votes in, 67–69, 73; powers of, 114–15; passes assumption bill, 118, 119; approves Eleventh Amendment, 119; charters Bank of the United States, 119–20; passes Alien and Sedition Acts, 120; nationalism of, after War of 1812, p. 126; enacts high tariff laws, 127; concurrent majority in, 132
Connecticut: suffrage in, 167
Conscription, 154, 156, 157–59
Constitution: defined, 81
Constitution, Confederate: as expression of southern desires, xix–xx; resemblance to U.S. Constitution, xx, 142; revolutionary purpose of, 79; drafted, 141; provisional, 141, 148; provisions of, 142–46, 182; ratification of, 146–47; provides for supreme court, 149; taxation provisions, 155; praised, 183; and funding law, 185
Constitution, U.S.: resemblance of Confederate Constitution to, xx, 142; associated with rebellion, 79; amendment of, 86–87, 119; religious tests forbidden in, 88; and reaction against legislative supremacy, 95; installed by state conventions, 111; federalism in, 113–18; broad construction of, 114–15; supremacy clause in, 116–17; strict construction of, 120, 127; Calhoun's interpretation of, 130; becomes bulwark of slavery, 135–36; southern attitude toward, 142
Constitutional amendments proposed in 1861, xvi
Constitutional convention: invented, 82; as embodiment of sovereignty, 111–12
Constitutional Convention, Confederate: revolutionary purpose of, 79; drafts provisional and permanent constitutions, 141; as provisional Congress, 148; continues U.S. laws, 152; and supreme court, 103–104
Constitutional Convention, U.S.: adopts three-fifths compromise, 10, 92; designs federal system, 114–18; and judicial review, 115–16; and restraint of states, 116; and concurrent majority, 132
Constitutional conventions, southern: ratify Confederate Constitution, 147. *See also* individual states
Constitutionalism: state constitutions original models of, xvii; defined, 81; and constitutional con-

vention, 82; in Confederacy, 160; in sectional argument, 174. *See also* States-rights constitutionalism
Constitutions, English, 79
Constitutions, southern: development of xvii–xviii, 80, 84–85, 164; amendment of, 86–87; popular participation in writing of, 87; suffrage and officeholding qualifications in, 88–90; representation in, 91–94; and structure of state government, 95–98, 170, 171; and judicial review, 98–102, 172, 172–73, 174; and bills of rights, 101–102, 174; and local government, 102–104, 175; superlegislation in, 105–106; education in, 106–107; slavery in, 107–108, 176; democratic tendencies in, 108–109; imitativeness of, 109. *See also* individual states.
Constitutions, state: scholarship on, xvii, 82–83; framing of, 81–82, 83–84, 163; submission of, to people, 84–85; written from 1800 to 1860, p. 85; revision of, 86–87, 165; property and religious qualifications in, 88; lengthening of, 104–105; limit state authority, 114; due process clauses in, 174. *See also* Constitutions, southern; and individual states
Constitutions, written, 79, 82, 109, 147–48
Convention format: nonconstitutional uses of, 110–11
Cooper, William J., Jr., 75
Counties, southern, 103

County courts, 103–104, 175
County offices, 103–104, 175
Court of claims, 144, 155
Courts, southern. *See* Judiciary, southern; Judiciary, Confederate
Craven, Avery O., 1–2, 3, 6–7, 51
Currency, Confederate, 154, 156
Cushing, Caleb, 45

Daniel, John M., 137–38
Dartmouth College v. Woodward, 126
Davis, David Brion, 4
Davis, Jefferson: on causes of Civil war, 26; in Buchanan's cabinet, 45–46; on secession as last resort, 60–61; proposes enlistment of slaves, 138; on Confederate Constitution, 142; reelected president, 148; and Confederate Supreme Court, 149, 150–51; vetoes by, 151; and opinions of attorneys general, 152; disagrees with Stephens, 154; calls for direct taxes, 155–56; requests habeas corpus suspension, 157
Declaration of rights, state, 101–102
Degler, Carl N., 3
Delaware: and Missouri Compromise, 19; suffrage in, 90, 167; representation in, 92
Delaware constitution: drafted by convention, 84; rejected in 1853, p. 85; revision process in, 86, 87; religious test removed from, 88; property qualification for office in, 89; lengthening of, 104–105; separation of powers in, 169–70; slavery not protected in, 176. *See also* Delaware

Democratic party: southern, and secession, xv; bisectional character of, 30; and popular sovereignty, 39; wins election of 1852, pp. 45, 47; as defender of South, 45, 46–47; southern control of, 46–47, 134; survival of 47–48; under cross-pressures, 48–49; split by Lecompton struggle, 55; in elections of 1856 and 1858, p. 58; division in, 58–62
DeVoto, Bernard, 2
District of Columbia: slavery in, xiii, 34, 135; slave trade in, xiii, xiv, 41, 68–69
Divorce, 86, 105
Donald, David Herbert, 2
Dorr, Thomas, 111
Douglas, Stephen A.: and popular sovereignty, 38–39; and Compromise of 1850, p. 41; on Compromise of 1850, p. 43; and South, 48, 56, 59–62; and Kansas-Nebraska Act, 51; heads anti-Lecompton movement, 55
Dred Scott decision, xviii, 39, 59, 64, 136
Dueling, 105
Due process clause, 101, 174

Eaton, Clement, 9
Education: in southern constitutions, 106–107
Edwards, Ninian, 20
Elazar, Daniel J., xviii
Elections: of 1796, p. 11; of 1800, p. 122; of 1852, pp. 45, 47, 64; of 1856, xiv, 57–58; of 1858, xiv, 58; of 1860, xv, 62, 64, 136, 145; of 1861 (Confederate), 148. *See also* Suffrage
Eleventh Amendment, 119
Embargo, 122
English compromise, 55, 59
Ex post facto clause, 101, 174

Faulkner, Charles J., 31–32
Federal government: powers of, 113; southern dominance in, 133–35
Federalism: in British empire, 113; in U.S. Constitution, 113–18; defined on battlefield, 118; in Confederate Constitution, 143
Federalist, The, 113
Federalist party, 10–11, 13, 14, 120–23
Fifth Amendment, 32
Fillmore, Millard, 58
Florida: secession of, 5; and Compromise of 1850, p. 42; representation in 93, 168, 169; financial provisions of constitution, 106; local government in, 175
Floyd, John B., 183
Foner, Eric, 2–3
Foote, Henry S., 33
Fort Sumter, ix, xvi, 65
Freeport doctrine, 59
Free Soil party, 64
Frémont, John C., 58
Fugitive-slave acts, xii, 32, 68–69
Fugitive slaves, 32–33, 133, 135–36
Funding law, Confederate, 156, 185

Garrison, William Lloyd, 30–31, 129–30
Gaston, William, 88–89
Georgia: secession of, 5; and Com-

promise of 1850, p. 42; disunionism in, 44; suffrage in, 90; representation in, 92, 93, 168, 168–69; limits judicial tenure, 98, 172; local government in, 103, 104, 175; and *Chisholm v. Georgia,* 118–19; and nullification, 131; defies U.S. Supreme Court, 131; opposition to Davis policies in, 156–57, 158, 159, 185; judges elected in, 172
Georgia Constitution: drafted by convention, 84; revised, 84; ratification process, 85; amendments to, 86; religious test removed from, 88; property qualifications for office removed from, 166–67; separation of powers in, 169; executive veto in, 170; on judicial review, 172; slavery not protected in, 176. *See also* Georgia
Georgia platform, 7, 53, 72
Georgia supreme court: established, 86, 165; upholds impressment, 159
Geyl, Pieter, 2
Governor: powers of, 95, 96; election of, 96
Green, Fletcher M., 83
Green, John W., 173
Guadalupe Hidalgo, Treaty of, 35

Habeas corpus, writ of: suspension of, in Confederacy, 154, 156–59, 185, 186
Haiti, xiii, 129
Hamilton, Alexander: financial program of, 10; on bills of rights, 101; on national bank, 114–15, 151; on judicial review, 115–16; proposes assumption of state debts, 118; proposes Bank of the United States, 119–20
Hammond, James H., 135, 141–42
Harrisburg, Pa., tariff convention, 127
Hartford Convention, 123
Harpers Ferry, 6, 7, 52, 62
Hill, Benjamin H., 150
Holt, Michael F., 75
Hunter v. Martin, 124, 179
Hurst, James Willard, 106

Illinois: slavery in, 13; and elections of 1856 and 1858, p. 58
Impeachment: in Confederate Constitution, 143
Impressment of supplies, 154, 159
Imprisonment for debt, 105
Incorporation: in southern constitutions, 105–106; congressional power of, 114–15
Indiana: slavery in, 13; and elections of 1856 and 1858, p. 58
Internal improvements, 34; in Confederate Constitution, 143
Iowa: admission of, 29
Item veto: in Confederate Constitution, 144

Jackson, Andrew, 131
Jacksonian democracy, xviii
Jay's treaty, 10
Jefferson, Thomas: and southern sectionalism, 10–12; on Missouri crisis, 14; effort of, to ban slavery in trans-Appalachian West, 35; and legislative supremacy, 95; on de-

pendent judges, 96; on county courts, 103; and assumption bill, 118; opposes Bank of the United States, 120, 151; and Virginia and Kentucky Resolutions, 120–22; and constitutionality of Louisiana Purchase, 122; and majoritarian politics, 125; Calhoun compared to, 127–28; on constitutional revision, 165
Jews: admitted to electorate in Maryland, 166
Johnson, Andrew, 132
Judicial review: categories of, xviii; emergence of, 82; in southern state courts, 98–102, 172, 172–73, 173; reliance of framers on, 115
Judiciary, Confederate, 148–51, 153–54, 158–59, 183–84
Judiciary, southern: made elective, xvii–xviii, 97–98, 171–72; tenure of, xvii–xviii, 98, 172; judicial review in, xviii, 98–102, 172–73, 174; independence partly achieved, 96–97, 170, 171. *See also* Judiciary, Confederate
Judiciary Act of 1789, pp. 117, 177–78
Justice in Grey (Robinson), 153

Kansas: admission of, 50, 56; as southern bane, 64
Kansas-Nebraska Act: repeals Missouri Compromise restriction, xiv, 18, 22; as extension of Compromise of 1850, pp. 43, 51; consequences of, 49; and southern expansionism, 50; southern motives and, 51–53; symbolic victory for South, 53; effect of, on party system, 56, 136
Kansas Territory: violence in, 52
Kearny, Stephen W., 34
Kentucky: and secession, 5; and Missouri Compromise, 19; suffrage in, 89; court controversy in, 97; judicial review in, 101; in Confederacy, 147; judicial system of, 171; local government in, 175
Kentucky constitution: in 1790s, 84; revision process in, 87; provisions for local government in, 104; and slavery, 107, 108; derivation of, 109. *See also* Kentucky
Kinsey, Charles, 20
Knox, Henry, 116
Know-Nothing (American) party, 56, 58

Lamar, John B., 26
Lecompton controversy, xiv, 52, 53–56, 58, 59, 65, 76
Lee, Robert E., 158
Legal tender legislation, 156
Legislative apportionment. *See* Representation
Legislative supremacy, xvii, 95, 99
Lincoln, Abraham, ix–x, xv, 59, 62, 64
Local government, southern, 102–104, 174, 174–75, 175
Lotteries, 105
Louisiana: secession of, 5; and Compromise of 1850, p. 42; suffrage in, 90, 167; representation in, 93, 168; judicial system of, 171; local government in, 174, 175
Louisiana constitution: and ed-

ucation, 106–107; derivation of, 109; property qualifications for office removed from, 166–67; slavery not protected in, 175. *See also* Louisiana

Louisiana Purchase: slavery in, 12, 28, 36; constitutionality of, 122

Lower South: creates Confederacy, xv; secession of, xv, 46, 64; defined, 5–6; and Missouri Compromise, 19, 42; conditional unionism in, 44; collapse of Whig party in, 48; and African slave trade, 56; and Douglas, 59, 61; and Lecompton issue, 76

McCulloch v. Maryland, 124, 126

McGrath, Andrew G., 154

Madison, James: quoted on slavery, ix; and Missouri controversy, 14; and U.S. Constitution, 82; and legislative supremacy, 95; on federal system, 113; favors congressional veto of state laws, 116; and assumption bill, 118; opposes Bank of the United States, 119–20; and Virginia and Kentucky Resolutions, 120–22; curbs resistance to *U.S. v. Peters*, 123; on Hartford Convention, 123; and majoritarian politics, 125; presidential policies of, 126; suggests sectional representation in Congress, 132

Marbury v. Madison, xviii

Maine: admission of, 15, 17, 18

Manumission, 107

Married women's property, 105

Marshall, John, 99, 123, 124, 153

Martial law: in Confederacy, 156

Martin v. Hunter's Lessee, 126, 179

Maryland: and Missouri Compromise, 19; fugitive slaves of, 32; suffrage in, 90; representation in, 92, 93, 168; powers of governor in, 95, 170; judicial review in, 99; local government in, 103, 174–75; judicial system of, 171, 172

Maryland constitution: drafted by convention, 84; revision process in, 86; religious test in, 88, 166; property qualifications in, 89; declaration of rights in, 101; provisions in, for local government, 104; bans imprisonment for debt, 105; fixes maximum interest, 105; property qualifications for office removed from, 166; separation of powers in, 169; slavery in, 176. *See also* Maryland

Mason, James M., 32, 33, 107

Massachusetts: constitution of 1780, p. 84, 91, 163; suffrage in, 167

Mering, John V., 49

Mexican Cession, 35, 36, 38, 40

Mexican War, 34

Middle South: and secession, xv–xvi; defined, 6; conditional unionism in, 44; and Lecompton issue, 76

Militia service: as qualification for suffrage, 167

Mississippi: secession of, 5; and Compromise of 1850, p. 42; disunionism in, 44; suffrage in, 90, 167; local government in, 104, 175; and married women's property, 105; representation in, 169

Mississippi constitution: elective supreme court in, xvii–xviii, 97–98; judicial tenure in, xvii–xviii, 98; religious test in, 88; ordinariness of, 109; removes property qualifications for office, 166. *See also* Mississippi

Mississippi convention of 1832, pp. 97–98

Missouri: and secession, 5; admission of, 14–15, 18, 29, 36, 42; constitution of 1846 rejected by voters, 85; in Confederacy, 147; taxpaying qualification for legislature in, 166; representation in, 168; judicial system, 171; local government in, 175

Missouri Compromise, xiii, 15, 17–19, 29, 38, 42–43

Missouri Compromise restriction (36° 30' line): resolves territorial issue, xiii; repeal of, xiv, 50, 51; passed, 15, 18–20; southern support of, 26; southern attitudes toward, 29, 129, 136; extension of, proposed, 37–38; as badge of southern inferiority, 52–53; votes on, 67–69, 73

Missouri controversy (1819–21), xi, xii; as turning point, 9–10, southern role in, 13–23; compared with Wilmot Proviso struggle, 36; and change in southern outlook, 128–29, 133

Missouri Territory: organized, 28

Mobile *Register and Advertiser,* 183

Modernization, 3–4

Monroe, James, 14, 17

Montgomery convention. *See* Constitutional Convention, Confederate

Moore, Albert Burton, 153

Moore, Glover, 18, 19, 20, 21

Nashville convention, 40

Negroes, free, 15, 16, 32

Nevins, Allan, 2

New Hampshire: constitution of 1784, pp. 84, 91, 163; suffrage in, 167

New Jersey: in elections of 1856 and 1858, p. 58; suffrage in, 167

New Mexico: proposed admission of, 39–40

New Mexico Territory: organized, 41, 68–69

New York: slavery in, 13; popular ratification of state constitution, 85

Nicholas, Wilson Cary, 122

Nichols, Roy F., 2

Nieman, Donald, 145

Nonintervention, 28, 43

North Carolina: secession of, 5; constitutional convention of 1835 in, 88–89; suffrage in, 90, 167; representation in, 92, 93, 168; constitutional conservatism in, 94; taxation of slaves in, 94, 108; judicial review in, 101; ratifies Confederate Constitution, 147; opposition to Jefferson Davis' policies in, 156, 158–59

North Carolina constitution: drafted by convention, 84; amendment of, 85–86; religious test in, 88–89, 166; property qualifications for office in, 89; separation of pow-

ers in, 169; slavery not protected in, 175. *See also* North Carolina
Northwest Ordinance, xii, xiii, 16, 28
Nullification: studies of, xi; by a state convention, 111; in Kentucky Resolutions, 121; in South Carolina "Exposition," 127; Calhoun and, 127, 179, 180; by South Carolina, 130, 131; not authorized in Confederate Constitution, 143; and states-rights theory, 160

Officeholding: made elective, xvii, 90–91; property qualifications for, 88, 89, 166–67; religious tests for, 88–89, 166; taxpaying qualifications for, 166
Ohio: suffrage in, 167
Oregon: as Democratic state, 50
Oregon Territory: organization of, 35, 37, 38; as part of Compromise of 1850, p. 42
Oregon Treaty, 34
Orleans Territory: slavery in, 13
Outman, George W., 1
Overton, Frank L., 172–73
Owsley, Frank L., 2, 160–61, 186

Pearson, Richmond M., 158–59
Pennsylvania: personal liberty law of, 32; in elections of 1856 and 1858, p. 58; representation in, 91; resists *U.S. v. Peters*, 123–24; hostility to *McCulloch v. Maryland* in, 124; suffrage in, 167
Personal liberty laws, 32
Peterson, Merrill, 122
Pierce, Franklin, 45, 47, 57, 137, 141

Pinckney, Charles, 116
Political parties: and southern power, xix; southern hostility to, xx, 145; and the constitutional system, 110; emergence of, 120. *See also* individual parties
Polk, James K., 34
Popular consent, 87–88
Popular sovereignty, 28, 38–39, 43, 87
Potter, David M., 2, 64, 139
Presidency, Confederate: in Confederate Constitution, 144–46
Presidency, U.S.: proposed changes in, 132
Property qualifications: for suffrage, 87, 88, 89–90, 93, 167; for officeholding, 88, 89, 166–67
Public finance: in southern constitutions, 105–106; in Confederacy, 155–56, 185

Quitman, John A., 97–98

Randall, James G., 2
Randolph, Edmund, 95, 120
Reid, Robert, 23
Religious qualifications for officeholding and suffrage, 88–89, 166
Representation, 91–94, 167, 168–69
Republican ideology (republicanism), x–xi, xviii, xx, 145–46
Republican party: birth of, xiv–xv, 4, 56–57; aided by Lecompton controversy, 55, 56; southern view of, 57; in elections of 1856 and 1858, p. 58; southern fear of, 62–63; captures presidency, 63, 64
Republican party (Jeffersonian),

10–14, 30, 120–22, 134
Residence requirements, 90, 167
Rhett, Robert Barnwell, 134
Rhode Island: Dorr Rebellion in, 111; suffrage in, 167
Richmond *Enquirer,* 19–20, 21, 35, 63, 123, 141
Richmond *Examiner,* 137–38
Robinson, William M., Jr., 153
Russel, Robert R., 43

Schlesinger, Arthur M., Jr., 2
Secession: explanation of, ix, 4–7; republican ideology and, xi; and southern disunity, xv; by state conventions, 112; Calhoun and, xix, 130–31; purpose of, 138, 142; and southern nationalism, 138–41; and states-rights theory, 140; not provided for in Confederate Constitution, 143, 182; a formal process, 160; expected to be peaceable, 182. *See also* Secessionism
Secessionism: in 1819–21, xii, 20–21; in 1850, pp. 25–26, 44; in 1856, xiv; in 1858, pp. 53–54, 55; in 1856, p. 57; in 1860–61, xvi, 60–61, 63–64. *See also* Secession
Sellers, Charles G., 52
Separation of powers, 95–96, 169–70
Sequestration law, Confederate, 154–55
Seward, William H., 33, 39
Shorter, Eli S., 22
Sickles, Daniel, 140
Silbey, Joel H., 2
Slavery: centrality of, ix–x; defines and unifies South, x, xv; in Missouri controversy, xii–xiii, 13–23, 128–29; in District of Columbia, xiii, 34, 135; in crisis of 1846–50, xiii–xiv, 26–44; and Kansas, xiv, 49–56; and rise of Republican party, xv, 56–57; in secession crisis, xvi, 62–63; in Confederate Constitution, xx; as early issue, 10; in Jeffersonian period, 11–12; moral argument about, 22–23; territorial code for, demanded, 59–60, 62; and representation, 92–93, 168, 169; in Virginia convention of 1829–30, p. 93; and fear of majority rule, 94; in southern judicial review, 100; controversy over, and southern education, 107; in southern constitutions, 107–108, 176; and problem of federalism, 113; abolished in British West Indies, 130; protection needed by, 133; and "doughface" factor in politics, 134; U.S. Constitution becomes bulwark of, 135–36; as reason for secession, 138; in Confederate Constitution, 142–43; effect of Civil War on, 160. *See also* Slaves; Slave trade
Slaves: fugitive, 32–33, 133, 135–36; taxation of, 94, 108, 169
Slave trade: African, xii, 56; in District of Columbia, xiii, xiv, 41, 68–69
Smith, William, 22
Snyder, Simon, 123
South: Civil War and characterization of, ix; slavery and characterization of, ix–x; scholarship on,

x–xi; as abstraction, xv; constitutional development in, xvii–xviii; constitutional theory in, xviii–xix; political power of, xix, 11, 29–30, 45–46, 133–35; as distinct section, 9–10; committed to permanency of slavery, 23, 44; empty victories of, 64–65; as conscious minority, 125, 128. *See also* Border South; Confederate South; Lower South; Middle South; and individual southern states

South Carolina: secession of, 5; and Missouri Compromise, 19; declares causes of secession, 33; and Compromise of 1850, p. 42; disunionism in, 44; as category by itself, 71; religious test in, 88; 166; suffrage in, 88, 90, 91; property qualifications for office in, 89; representation in, 91, 167, 168; powers of governor in, 95, 170; legislative supremacy in, 96; punishes judges, 97; as exception to democratization, 108; supports assumption bill, 119; nationalism in, 124; states-rights revolution in 126–28; Vesey plot in, 129; nullification by, 130, 131; ratifies Confederate Constitution, 146–47; judicial system of, 170, 171; local government in, 174, 174–75; favors secession clause in Confederate Constitution, 182

South Carolina constitution: an exception, xvii; drafted by legislature, 84; revisions of, 87; separation of powers in, 169–70; slavery not protected in, 175. *See also* South Carolina

South Carolina "Exposition," 127

Southern nationalism, xx, 138–40, 142, 143–44, 146, 181

Stampp, Kenneth M., 2, 139

State constitutions. *See* Constitutions, state; Constitutions, southern; and individual states

State governments: powers of 113–14

State offices: made elective, xvii, 90–91

State sovereignty: theory of, xix; in Confederate Constitution, 143

States-rights constitutionalism, xii, xix, 125–29, 160–61

Staunton, Va.: conventions at, 111

Stephens, Alexander H.: on constitutional causes of Civil War, xvi; threatens disunion, 35, 40; defends Compromise of 1850, pp. 42–43; on southern dominance of federal government, 46, 133–34; as reluctant secessionist 154; opposes Davis policies, 156–57

Suffrage: property qualifications for, 87, 88, 89–90, 167; religious test for, in South Carolina, 88, 166; taxpaying qualifications for, 88, 89–90, 167; residence requirements for, 90, 167; sectional differences in, 90; in Virginia convention of 1829–30, pp. 93–94; militia service and, 167

Supremacy clause, 116–17

Supreme Court, Confederate, 149–51, 183–84

Supreme Court, U.S.: southern majority on, 30, 46; and popular sovereignty, 39; Dred Scott decision of, xviii, 39, 59, 64, 136; power of, to review state court decisions, 117, 177–78; decision in *Chisholm v. Georgia*, 119; decision in *U.S. v. Peters*, 123; decision in *McCulloch v. Maryland*, 124; nationalist decisions of, 126; defied by Georgia, 131; protects slavery, 135–36 Supreme courts, southern: establishment of, 96–97; attacks on, 97; made elective, 97–98, 171–72; tenure of, 98. *See also* Judicial review

Sydnor, Charles S., 9

Tallmadge, James, Jr., 14
Tallmadge amendment: and Missouri Compromise, 14–15, 17, 128–29; and Arkansas, 16; and gradual abolition, 22; compared to Wilmot Proviso, 22; voting on, 67, 69, 73; defeated in Senate, 132
Taney, Roger B., 63, 136
"Tariff of abominations," 127
Taxation: of slaves, 94, 108, 169; Confederate, 154, 155–56
Taxpaying qualifications, 88, 89–90, 166, 167
Taylor, John, 122
Taylor, John W., 18
Taylor, Zachary, 39, 40, 47, 61
Tennessee: Civil War battlefields in, xv; secession of, 5; 1859 election in, 49; fear of majority rule in, 94; powers of governor in, 96; judicial system of, 98, 170, 171; taxation of slaves in, 108; submits Confederate Constitution to voters, 147; property qualifications for officeholding abolished in, 166; suffrage in, 167; representation in, 168; local government in, 175
Tennessee constitution: drafted, 84; revision process in, 87; religious test in, 88, 166; derivation of, 109. *See also* Tennessee
Texas: secession of, 5; annexation of, 33–34; boundary claims of, 39, 41; admission of, 53; married women's property in, 105; financial provisions of constitution, 105–106; education in, 106; representation in, 168; judicial system of, 171–72; local government in, 175
Thomas, Emory M., 139
Thomas, Jesse B., 20
Thornton, J. Mills, xi
Three-fifths compromise, 92, 168, 168–49
Toombs, Robert, 25, 26, 27, 31, 140
Trescot, William B., 134
Turnbull, Robert J., 129
Turner, Nat, 129
Tyler, John, 16

Upper South: defined, 6
Upshur, Abel P., 93
U.S. v. Peters, 123
Utah Territory: organized, 41, 68–69

Vance, Zebulon B., 158
Venable, Abraham W., 26
Vesey, Denmark, 22, 129
Veto: in southern constitutions, 95,

96, 170; of state laws by Congress proposed, 116; Jefferson Davis' use of, 151
Virginia: secession of, 5; early talk of secession in, 11; and Missouri Compromise, 19; fugitive slaves of, 32; suffrage in, 90, 93, 167; representation in 92, 93–94, 168; constitutional conservatism in, 94; judicial review in, 100, 101, 172, 173; local government in, 103, 104; taxation of slaves in, 108; denounces assumption bill, 118; and U.S. Supreme Court, 124; states-rights feeling in, 125–26; Nat Turner uprising in, 129; ratifies Confederate Constitution, 147; judicial system of, 171
Virginia and Kentucky Resolutions, 11, 120–22, 125, 126, 127
Virginia constitution: drafted by legislature, 84; popular ratification of, 85; property qualifications in, 89; drafted in 1830, pp. 93–94; drafted in 1851, p. 94; declaration of rights in, 101; separation of powers in, 169. *See also* Virginia
Virginia Plan, 116, 126
Voting. *See* Suffrage

Walker, Freeman, 21
Walker, Richard W., 173
Walker, Robert J., 50, 61
Washington, George, 120
Watts, Thomas Hill, 149–50, 153–54, 158
Weare, Kenneth, 79
Why the South Lost the Civil War (Beringer et al.), 139
Whig party: bisectional character of, 30; disintegration of, 47–48, 49, 56
Wilmot, David, 29, 34
Wilmot Proviso, 32, 40; southern reaction to, xiii–xiv; inaugurates crisis, 25–26, 29; Tallmadge amendment compared to, 22; struggle over, 34–36; alternatives to, 37–38; northern support of, 39; rejected in Compromise of 1850, pp. 43, 44; defeated in Senate, 132
Wisconsin: admission of, 29
Wood, Fernando, 140
Wood, Gordon, 81
Woodburn, James A., 9
Wooster, Ralph A., 175

Yancey, William Lowndes, 150, 184